THE CATHOLIC BIBLICAL QUARTERLY MONOGRAPH SERIES

5

MATTHEW

A SCRIBE TRAINED FOR THE KINGDOM OF HEAVEN

by

O. Lamar Cope

MATTHEW

A SCRIBE TRAINED FOR THE KINGDOM OF HEAVEN

BY

O. LAMAR COPE

Carroll College

Waukesha, Wisconsin

PICKWICK *Publications*

An imprint of *Wipf and Stock Publishers*

Pickwick Publications
An imprint of Wipf and Stock Publishers
199 W 8th Ave, Suite 3
Eugene, OR 97401

Matthew
A Scribe Trained for the Kingdom of Heaven
By Cope, O. Lamar

Softcover ISBN-13: 978-1-6667-7997-4
Hardcover ISBN-13: 978-1-6667-7998-1
eBook ISBN-13: 978-1-6667-7999-8
Publication date 5/8/2023
Previously published by The Catholic Biblical Association of America, 1976

This edition is a scanned facsimile of the original edition published in 1976.

To Virginia, faithful friend.

TABLE OF CONTENTS

PREFACE

This book is an inquiry into the possibility and consequences of a controlled investigation of the work of one of the Gospel writers. Its primary thrust is methodological because it asks how we can identify the work of the final author/editors with any degree of clarity. The model application of the method revolves around the use of the Old Testament by the author of the Gospel of Matthew. The study is published here essentially as it was prepared as a doctoral dissertation at Union Theological Seminary and completed in 1971. In a few cases literature that has subsequently appeared has been considered but no attempt has been made at a complete revision nor is there any intention that the study represent a complete listing of critical literature on Matthew. Instead, it invites the reader to follow a tracing of clues to the work of the author of the Gospel and to consider also their implications.

A number of persons deserve grateful mention for their help along the way. Their number includes a score of teachers who have probed, prompted, and provoked thought at both Union Theological Seminary and Wesley Theological Seminary. Dr. J. Louis Martyn has been both an unflagging source of help and encouragement and a critic requiring accuracy in method, form, and content. Drs. Reginald H. Fuller, Walter Wink, and James Sanders were also of great help. Dr. Thomas Longstaff's interest and effort was an immense resource. Special thanks are due to my wife, Sandra, for typing the initial draft and to Miss Virginia Hamner for typing the final draft.

Grateful acknowledgement is also due to the members of the CBQMS editorial board and staff who have made this publication possible. The Very Rev. Thomas O. Barrosse, C.S.C., worked through the manuscript with care. Rev. Msgr. Patrick W. Skehan has continued with the editing of this monograph beyond his official term of office and through considerable technical difficulties. His skill, advice, and counsel have been freely given and deeply appreciated. Fr. Joseph Jensen has also seen the manuscript through a number of trials and is to be commended for his patience and competence.

Wherever possible the Revised Standard Version is employed for biblical citations. In a few cases a more literal translation has seemed necessary to illustrate the structure employed by the Matthean author.

Carroll College, Waukesha, Wisconsin / April 1975 L.C.

CHAPTER 1

INTRODUCTION

In recent years the study of the Synoptic Gospels has turned markedly in the direction of redaction criticism.* The search for the special purposes and motifs which guided the gospel writers has now become one of the most important and exciting realms of NT studies. The present surge of interest in redaction criticism stems from the ground-breaking study of Luke by Hans Conzelmann which was published in 1953 as *Die Mitte der Zeit.*[1] Since this book's appearance there has been a steadily growing awareness that the role of the writers of the gospels, both in their function of editing the original traditions and as creative authors in their own right, is vitally important for an adequate critical understanding of these documents. The task of redaction criticism is that of discovering the distinctive situations, purposes, approaches and theologies of the writers who gave the gospels their final shape.

Although Conzelmann's work opened new vistas of inquiry, he made no systematic effort to define a method by which the work of an author such as Luke might be discovered. Willi Marxsen, in his *Der Evangelist Markus,*[2] however, defined more carefully the realm of inquiry encompassed by redaction criticism. He described three stages in the process of the growth of the gospels. The first stage was that of the life and teachings of Jesus. The second stage was the growth of the oral tradition in the early church. The third stage, which has not been adequately explored, is the writing of a complete gospel by a particular writer in a particular situation.[3] In this way, Marxsen attempted to distinguish the special province of redaction criticism. But Marxsen, like Conzelmann, did not go on to establish a clear method for separating the work of the writer from the traditions used by him.

*There have been a number of surveys of redaction critical study. A good report about the critique of the work done thus far is given by R. H. Stein, "What is Redaktionsgeschichte?" *JBL* 88 (1969) 45-56. A more extensive report but one deficient in methodological critique is *Rediscovering the Teaching of the Evangelists,* by Joachim Rohde, trans. by Dorothea Barton (London: SCM Press, 1968). A similar deficiency affects the work of Norman Perrin, *What is Redaction Criticism?* (Philadelphia: Fortress Press, 1969).

1. Available in English as *The Theology of St. Luke,* trans. by G. Buswell (London: Faber & Faber, 1960).

2. *Der Evangelist Markus. Studien zur Redaktionsgeschichte des Evangeliums* (Göttingen: Vandenhoeck and Ruprecht, 1956). This work is now available in English as *Mark the Evangelist,* trans. by Roy A. Harrisville [*et al.*] (Nashville: Abingdon Press, 1969).

3. Marxsen, *Der Evangelist Markus,* 12. Stein, in "What is Redaktionsgeschichte?" 49, correctly stresses the importance of the very fact of the writing of the gospels. This is an important event in the transmission of the tradition and merits full critical attention.

The heightened interest in the writers of the gospels as whole documents has also stimulated a great deal of work on the Gospel of Matthew. R. Hummel and W. D. Davies have studied the relationship of Matthew and his church to the contemporary Jewish world.[4] The special theological stiuation of Matthew in the early church is the subject of a work coauthored by G. Bornkamm, G. Barth, and H. J. Held.[5] Both W. Trilling and G. Strecker have explored the relationship of Matthew to the emerging Gentile church.[6] The early work of K. Stendahl and the recent study by R. Grundy have concentrated on the role of the Old Testament citations in the gospel.[7]

The most striking result of these labors is the diversity of critical conclusions.[8] Stendahl proposed that the setting for the gospel was a community of Scripture scholars similar to the one which existed at Qumran.[9] Although this work has been widely admired, it has not been widely accepted.[10] Davies and Hummel believe the author to have been a Jewish-Christian involved in an intense controversy with post-70 A.D. Pharisaic Judaism.[11] Strecker contends that the final author is a Gentile Christian thinking primarily of the Gentile mission.[12] Trilling stresses the ways in which Matthew seeks to chart a course for the nascent catholic church.[13]

How and why have such divergent opinions arisen and how can they be critically assessed? Answers to these questions are to be found in the widely varied presuppositions of the writers and in their conflicting methods of approach. This chaotic situation calls for a new approach to redaction analysis of Matthew. The major cause of the current confusion has been the lack of any definite, critically defensible way of separating tradition from

4. R. Hummel, *Die Auseinandersetzung zwischen Kirche und Judentum im Matthäusevangelium* (München: Chr. Kaiser Verlag, 1963) and W. D. Davies, *The Setting of the Sermon on the Mount* (Cambridge: Cambridge University Press, 1964).

5. G. Bornkamm, G. Barth, and H. J. Held, *Tradition and Interpretation in Matthew*, trans. P. Scott (London: SCM Press, 1963). The work appeared in German in 1960 as *Auslegung und Uberlieferung im Matthäusevangelium*.

6. W. Trilling, *Das wahre Israel* (2nd ed.; München: Kösel-Verlag, 1946) and G. Strecker, *Der Weg der Gerechtigkeit* (2nd ed.; Göttingen: Vandenhoeck & Ruprecht, 1966).

7. K. Stendahl, *The School of St. Matthew* (2nd ed.; Philadelphia: Fortress Press, 1968) originally appeared in 1954; R. Gundry, *The Use of the Old Testament in St. Matthew's Gospel* (Leiden: Brill, 1967).

8. This disparity is also plainly seen by K. Tagawa, "People and Community in the Gospel of Matthew," *NTS* 16 (1970) 149–162.

9. Stendahl, *School*, 201.

10. The "school hypothesis" has not been convincing because of the sense critics have had of a broader unity in theme of the gospel than such corporate authorship would suggest. However, not all of Stendahl's work hinges on this hypothesis. Used carefully, and supplemented by B. Gärtner's fine article, "The Habbakuk Commentary and the Gospel of Matthew," *ST* 8 (1954) 1–24, Stendahl's work is of pivotal importance.

11. Davies, *Sermon on the Mount*, 255, and Hummel, *Die Auseinandersetzung*, 9–10.

12. Strecker, *Der Weg*, 15–35.

13. Trilling, *Das wahre Israel*, 19.

Matthean redaction. As a result, work has been begun by the selection of redactional material without critically controlled methods of making the selection.[14]

A serious limitation of the current works on Matthean redaction is an inadequate definition of the scope of redactional inquiry. Far too often critics have been concerned with the seams, summaries, and insertions which have supposedly been made in reference to earlier tradition. Such evidence is an important element in redaction analysis, but these bits and pieces do not constitute the whole of the redactor's work. Therefore, a complete picture of the author's purposes and ideas cannot be gained by sole attention to such items. To use an analogy that has been popular among form critics, the gospels are like beads on a string. The redaction analyst seeks to understand the nature of the string and not simply to gather the bits of string that can be cut from between the beads. The task necessitates a broader view of redaction. As Stein urges, this vision must be "concerned with ascertaining the unique contribution to and understanding of the sources used by the evangelists. This will be found in their seams, interpretive comments, summaries, modifications of material, selection of material, omission of material, arrangement, introductions, conclusions, vocabulary, and christological titles."[15] In all of these regards the evangelist has no doubt shaped his gospel to suit his purposes. Thus, a comprehensive approach is necessary.

Another weakness of contemporary redaction criticism has been an undue stress on theological motifs. Conzelmann's success with this approach in his work on Luke has undoubtedly had a strong effect on other later efforts.[16] But an adequate picture of the work of a gospel writer must be broader than a resumé of his theological biases. It must encompass something of his literary craft and of his historical situation insofar as they are revealed in the gospel. A simple example may be seen in the fact that a theological analysis of the work of Luke does not reveal Luke's tendency to provide appropriate introductory settings for the parables of Jesus. A complete redaction analysis needs to include such literary data in order to provide an adequate picture of the way in which this particular writer handles the traditions.[17] If it is objected that such an item appears to be simply literary criticism, the response must be that the evangelists are, after all, writers, and we need a

14. Strecker, *Der Weg,* has most clearly recognized this problem even though his own method of selection is as arbitrary and uncontrolled as are the methods evident in the other studies, 1–35.

15. Stein, "Redaktionsgeschichte," 53.

16. Even Stein, after a careful methodological appraisal, finally resorts to a narrowly theological definition of the goal of redaction, "Redaktionsgeschichte," 54.

17. Among the parables which are given Lucan introductions are: "The Good Samaritan," "The Lost Sheep," "The Lost Coin," "The Lost Son," and "The Pharisee and the Tax-Collector." Interestingly, J. Jeremias, *The Parables of Jesus,* trans. S. Hooke (rev. ed.; New York: Charles Scribner's Sons, 1962), 96–102, does not discuss this Lucan trait in his section on the settings of the parables.

picture of their special writing style in order to discern their work and to establish firm evidence for more substantive conclusions about their theological attitudes. The tracing of the string through the beads must be done in a manner flexible enough to include several elements, theological motif being but one important factor among them.

The strong tendency to understand redaction criticism solely from the perspective of the authors' theologies has contributed to the erroneous view that redaction criticism is a development of the past fifteen years. The result has been a cutting away of any awareness of the roots of the study in earlier work. As early as 1927, H. J. Cadbury developed a schema for the task of following the work of Luke which has not been surpassed for clarity of insight into the problems of redaction criticism.[18] Cadbury delineated the following primary factors in composition: "accessible materials, conventional media of thought and expression, individuality, and the author's conscious purpose."[19] The formulation of an opinion about the work of an author is, according to Cadbury, dependent upon the critic's discernment of the interweaving of these factors. He insists that "the analytical task precedes the synthetic one."[20] The author's hand must be traced with great care before any comments can be made about his overall purposes, theology, or historical stiuation.

Contemporary redaction work has also been myopic about the applicability of the method in the NT. Rohde says, "the method of redaction criticism . . . is in principle applicable only to the Synoptic Gospels, including the Acts of the Apostles, and not to the Epistles."[21] Such a limitation is indefensible. It must completely ignore the very productive work that has been done in redaction analysis of the Gospel of John since the appearance of Bultmann's great commentary.[22] The extensive application of redaction-critical method to the Acts, where there are often no parallel sources for cross reference, also suggests a broader application of the method.[23] In reality the method of redaction criticism applies wherever an author has employed sources in the writing of his document. In the NT the method may

18. H. J. Cadbury, *The Making of Luke-Acts* (2nd ed.; London: SPCK, 1958), especially the brief chapter, "Factors in Composition," 12–17.

19. Cadbury, pp. 13–15.

20. Cadbury, p. 16.

21. Rohde, *Rediscovering the Teaching of the Evangelists*, 9.

22. R. Bultmann, *Das Evangelium des Johannes* (18th printing of the 1941 original; Göttingen: Vandenhoeck and Ruprecht, 1964). Since this work the debate concerning the scope and nature of the redactional work in John has been intense. See R. E. Brown, *The Gospel of John*, I (The Anchor Bible; New York; Doubleday, 1966), for a full discussion.

23. From the essay of M. Dibelius in 1923, "Stilkritisches zur Apostelgeschichte," available in English as "Style Criticism of the Book of Acts," in *Studies in the Acts of the Apostles*, trans. Mary Ling (London: SCM Press, 1956), to the commentary of E. Haenchen, *Die Apostelgeschichte* (Mayers Kommentar; Göttingen: Vandenhoeck & Ruprecht, 1961), an increasingly successful effort has been made to distinguish Luke's sources from his own work in Acts.

fruitfully be applied to all four gospels, Acts, the Deutero-Pauline epistles, and to the book of Revelation.

Recent redaction studies have also been hampered by a lack of clarity about the relationship of redaction criticism to source criticism and form criticism. Form criticism has, by and large, taken up its work from the foundations laid by the source critics, and its proponents have relied almost completely upon the two-document hypothesis as a working hypothesis. Even so, a careful reading of any one of the major form critical works of the last half-century will reveal that questions of relative earliness are judged pericope by pericope. The rules of transmission of the tradition may indicate that first one then another of the gospels preserves the earlier tradition.[24] In this manner form criticism staked out for itself a basically independent and self-contained realm of inquiry.

But redaction criticism has not developed this independence. Most of these studies have been based entirely upon the two-document hypothesis.[25] This means in practice that the redaction critic allows the source critic to do a major part of his work for him. Furthermore, those who have made such use of a source theory have not been aware that the judgments source critics inevitably have made about the work of the Synoptic writers have not been controlled by the criteria which validate redaction criticism. Moreover, this unquestioning reliance on the two-document hypothesis has come at a time when serious new questions have been raised about its validity.[26]

As a methodological starting point, therefore, at least some of the redaction analysis of the Synoptic Gospels today should be free of any particular source theory. To require otherwise would unduly limit the process of separating tradition from redaction. Instead of relying on a source

24. This basic independence of the two-source hypothesis in specific instances may be seen in the work of R. Bultmann. E. P. Sanders, *The Tendencies of the Synoptic Tradition* (Cambridge: Cambridge University Press, 1969), 290–292, lists at least 14 instances in which Bultmann, in *The History of the Synoptic Tradition*, trans. John Marsh (Oxford: Basil Blackwell, 1963), favors Mt, or Lk, or their common tradition over the Marcan form of a passage as preserving the more original tradition.

25. All of the recent studies of Matthew known to me have presupposed the two-document hypothesis.

26. W. R. Farmer, *The Synoptic Problem* (New York: Macmillan, 1964), has traced the development of the two-document hypothesis and the critical consensus supporting it with the result that the process is shown to have been less than scientific throughout, thus perhaps hiding fundamental logical errors. His own revival of the Griesbach hypothesis is, however, too simplistically stated to be compelling. E. P. Sanders, *The Tendencies of the Synoptic Tradition*, has tested the reliability of the criteria used to establish early and late in the tradition by both source and form critics and found them to be largely unreliable. The Mk-Q hypothesis appears to be most vulnerable at the point of defining Q (cf. T. R. Rosche, "The Words of Jesus and the Future of the 'Q' Hypothesis," *JBL* 79 (1960) 210–220), and in the logical puzzle of the phenomena of order (Farmer, "The Lachmann Fallacy," *NTS* 15 [1968] 441–442, and Sanders, "The Argument from Order and the Relationship Between Matthew and Luke," *NTS* 15 [1968] 249–261).

theory, the redaction analysis proposed here will seek to show from internal evidence the basic strands of an author's thought processes and style of argument, his literary craft, and the theological purposes for which he writes. This information, a factor which has not been fully taken into account in source criticism, ought then to be weighed in the light of source theories and either be corrected by them or serve as a corrective to them.

The interrelationship of form and redaction criticism is not as simple as the relationship of either to source criticism. Though the insights of form criticism are essential in recognition of the elements of tradition, redaction analysis cannot be bound by prior formal analysis in the study of any given pericope. The discovery of an author's thread of reasoning may mean that a new form and history are required for the passage. A rigid decision to use the results of form critical study as the basis for redaction analysis would limit the redaction critical process in the same way as would rigid reliance on a source theory.

Granted this measure of independence, redaction criticism must not be employed as a thing unto itself. The methods of each type of criticism form a part of the exegetical circle. They may be employed independently by any investigator at any given time, but their tasks and their results overlap because they deal with parts of one grand development. It is a mistake to conceive, as some have, of the interrelationship of the methods in pyramidal fashion with redaction criticism built upon form criticism and form criticism built upon source criticism. Instead the methods form interlocking rings within the overall task of exegesis.[27]

THE METHOD OF REDACTION ANALYSIS AND ITS CONTROLS

In view of the foregoing review of the task of redaction criticism, it is essential that a method be developed which is clear in its definition of the criteria by which the work of the gospel writers themselves may be discovered. The method should be flexible enough to encompass the full range of an author's own influence upon the composition of the gospel. It should proceed with a careful independence from the specific results of source and form criticism. And it should be controlled by internally demonstrable data.

The initial step in analyzing any passage is the construction of an outline of the different blocks of material which make up the passage. This is done through the utilization of the criteria by which form critics have learned to identify the different types of material in the gospels. It should always be clear that this is an initial step which makes no judgments about origins of the material but simply attempts to discern the general nature of the material

27. Neither Stein nor Rohde is able to clarify this important factor in methodology. Both view the methods in pyramidal fashion. See Rohde, *Rediscovering the Teaching of the Evangelists,* 10–11, and Stein, "Redaktionsgeschichte," 52–56.

at hand. A rigid separation, which assigned one portion to redaction, another to tradition, would imply that the investigator already knows what he actually intends to discover.

The second step in analyzing a passage consists of a careful linear reading. The investigator seeks to discover the logical links, the narrative flow, the connections which give the material its present form and order. In the beginning this reading will best be done without side reference to the Synoptic parallels. In this way preconceived notions of gospel relationships will have a minimal effect on the search for internal structure. If it were not for our long practiced habits of cross reference study of the Synoptics, this approach would need no defense. It is the method applied to any ancient text in the interpretative effort. It is the method which must be used in criticism of a text like the Gospel of John because there the investigator has little recourse to parallel material. The use of the same method for the Synoptics is simply to give the fullest possible range to the method of redaction criticism.[28]

The process of linear reading can be done fruitfully only when it is carefully controlled. Without such control, arbitrary judgments cannot be avoided.[29] The strongest control is the evidence of a demonstrable logical pattern of organization. A linear reading seeks to ascertain the flow of thought which produces the connectives and provides structure. At times this pattern may be formal as in a collection of sayings arranged around a theme. At times the pattern may be the logic of an argument. Or the keys to the structure of a passage may be found in the clues which show that the rationale for the placing of a pericope in its unique place is in the wording of the preceding passage. The measure of this type of evidence is the cogency and clarity of the proposed logical pattern.[30]

A corollary of this control deserves attention. Where a linear reading of the text reveals the presence of a style of argument that is known to us with some precision in a non-gospel tradition such as those of Rabbinic Judaism,

28. Opening Synoptic studies to this broader range requires recognition that the problems involved are not unique to the gospels or even to the NT. A major contribution has been made in OT studies by G. von Rad in his attention to the perspectives of the redactors (*Studies in Deuteronomy*, trans. G. Stalker [London: SCM Press, 1953], *Genesis*, trans. J. H. Marks [Philadelphia: Westminister Press, 1961], and *The Theology of the Old Testament*, 2 vols., trans. G. Stalker [New York: Harper Bros., 1962]). In non-Biblical studies, similar problems confront the student of Homer. See "The Homeric Question," by J. Davison in *A Companion to Homer*, ed. Wace and Stubbings (London: Macmillan, 1962), 234–268. Common to all such studies is the effort to establish the work of the redactors by linear reading.

29. An example of the dangers of uncontrolled redactional claim is the esthetic unity of Mt urged by B. C. Butler, *The Originality of St. Matthew* (Cambridge: Cambridge University Press, 1951), which is beyond critical testing.

30. An example of the technique of linear reading using a coherent pattern as a control may be seen in the analysis of Jn 9 by J. L. Martyn, *History and Theology in the Fourth Gospel* (New York: Harper and Row, 1968), 3–41.

Greek philosophy, or Roman law, the degree to which the gospel passage conforms to the external pattern will serve as a guide to the organization of the passage.[31]

Another means of control upon linear reading is the use of some demonstrable source in the formation of the passage being investigated. The great value of such a phenomenon for control of the separation of tradition from redaction helps to explain the desire of most investigators to use the Mk-Q hypothesis in this way. A much more sure source, especially in Matthew, is the OT. Where it is possible to trace the organization of a passage by tracing the special use of an OT citation or allusion, a very valuable key to linear reading is present.[32]

It cannot be said that such analysis is clearly redactional analysis. The linear reading may discover the structure of one of the author's sources rather than that introduced by the author himself. A further control is needed. That control is the one fundamental to all redaction criticism. Items are to be assigned to the final redactor when they exhibit his special vocabulary, ideas, style, or preference. These stylistic clues are to be gathered from a wide range of the material in the document but especially in the interpretative summaries, introductions, and comments which would be assigned to a final editor on any literary analysis. There may be characteristic ideas or phrases which appear more or less throughout a document. In Matthew, for example, the phrase "men will weep and gnash their teeth" occurs six times and in various kinds of contexts: in the context of a miracle story, in an interpretation of parables, in the conclusion to a parable, and in the final judgment scene. Such a characteristic has great claim to being a favorite phrase of Matthew. The strength is correspondingly greater where more than one such characteristic occur together. This traditional type of evidence of redaction may be combined with the evidence of structure gained by redaction analysis in several ways. Where the linear structure discovered in the analysis contains characteristics established as literary traits of the author, very firm evidence of the work of the redactor is gained. Where the structure discovered shares none of the characteristics of the author, the evidence points toward the author's following of his source or sources. Absence of an identifiable pattern, with or without signs of the author's work, will suggest that the author is employing a source lacking in pattern or that redactional evidence is simply not available in this instance.

31. A dramatic instance of the use of such an external pattern of thought by a NT writer has been discovered in Paul's use of an analogy to Roman testatory law to shape portions of Galatians and Romans (G. Taylor, "The Function of *Pistis Christou* is Galatians," *JBL* 85 [1966] 58–76.

32. An example of the control over redaction analysis that is afforded by an author's use of the OT can readily be seen in the work of P. Borgen on Jn 6:31–58. Borgen traces the careful use by the author of a precise midrashic pattern of interpretation of an OT text (*Bread from Heaven* [Leiden: Brill, 1965]).

In summary, a redaction analysis of any given passage proceeds by the construction of an initial form critical outline, a careful linear reading to discern the structure of the passage, and a testing of the results in the wider context of the gospel to see if the linear reading reveals evidence indicating the presence of the author's hand. The application of this method, governed by the stated controls, ought to provide access to at least a partial picture of the author's work as he shapes the traditions into his own unique gospel. Of course, the attempt to read over the shoulder of an ancient author is fraught with difficulty. There will be times when neither vocabulary nor style clearly betrays the writer's hand, when no discernible logic can be found, and when no external source is available as a control. There will be instances in which the author appears arbitrarily to have copied his sources or illogically to have inserted a bit of tradition into a strange context. Thus, the boundaries of linear reading lie with the scrutability or inscrutability of the writer's purposes and techniques.

The final step of a redaction analysis involves the drawing together of the results. A single analysis must be considered in the light of others. Each individual step and then the sum of the analyses must then be placed in the larger context of the study of the whole document. For the final goal of the enterprise is a portrait of the author's work and the discovery of his distinctive situation in, and contribution to, the history of early Christianity.

THE APPLICATION OF THE METHOD TO MATTHEW

The final goal just mentioned is, for the present at least, beyond the reach of Matthean studies. The lack of a critically established starting point and of an agreed upon and demonstrable set of Matthean characteristics means that redaction analysis of Matthew must be begun piece by piece, step by step, linear analysis by linear analysis.

Accordingly, I have sought a starting point, a critically controlled basis from which further analysis might proceed. To that end, I have directed my attention toward a tracing of the author's work in those sections of the gospel where I have been able to discover adequate material for controlled application of the method proposed above. The research was begun from the basis of Stendahl's study of the OT citations which appear in Matthew.[33] The initial question asked of the Matthean passages was, whether the OT texts are more than just fulfillment texts, perhaps also giving some clue as to the author's way of structuring his gospel. Step by step I began to discover that there are structural relationships between some of the OT citations and the material which surrounds them. From this base, particularly in view of the presence of the OT as a valuable control, I have developed the following study. If these analyses are able to provide a critically defensible approach to

33. Stendahl, *The School of St. Matthew.*

Matthew's redactional activity, then a basis will have been established for the further tracing of the author's hand by means of more extensive application of the proposed method of redaction to the parts of the gospel not covered in this study.[34]

A number of important new insights that bear on problems of form and source critical questions emerge in the analyses. In order to concentrate attention on the redaction analysis of Matthew, a discussion of these results has been minimized. However, they do provide material for further research into the interrelationship of the critical disciplines.

THE WORKING HYPOTHESIS

I propose to demonstrate the validity of the following proposition and to discuss its consequences.

The author of the gospel of Matthew, whom I shall simply call Matthew,[35] was a Jewish-Christian author thoroughly familiar with the OT and with Jewish traditions of its interpretation. He employed this knowledge as a key to the organization of a number of the parts of his gospel. In so doing, he revealed to his readers certain of his characteristic ideas and beliefs. He especially showed his understanding of the relationship between his Christian faith and the OT and the relationship of both to the problems of Christians of his own day. He was, therefore, "a scribe trained for the kingdom of heaven" (Mt 13:52).[36]

34. Although a number of Matthean redactional studies have appeared in recent years, only the study by Wm. Thompson, *Matthew's Advice to a Divided Çommunity* (Rome: Biblical Institute Press, 1970), adopts a methodology similar to the one proposed here.

35. In calling him Matthew I make no judgment about the actual person and whether or not he was a disciple of the historical Jesus.

36. My use of this phrase derives from the tracing of Matthew's work in ch. 13 (ch. 2, analysis 1 below). I do not mean that it can be shown that Matthew was actually a Jewish scribe or that he had been trained as one, although both might be true. I do think that Matthew would not have objected to this description of himself. As R. H. Fuller, *The New Testament in Current Study* (New York: Charles Scribner's Sons, 1962), says, "Matthew betrays his method in Matthew 13:52."

CHAPTER 2

MID-POINT TEXTS IN MATTHEW

The application of redaction-critical method to Matthew is very difficult. The disunity that is so apparent among contemporary critics on questions of Matthean redaction is a direct reflection of the complex character of the gospel itself.[1] Not only does Matthew lack the kind of clue to his intentions that Luke gives in Lk 1:1–4 and in 24:44–52; Acts 1:1–11, but there are contradictory elements within Matthew which appear to be unresolved. Jesus and his disciples break the Sabbath laws (Mt 12:1–14), but "whoever relaxes the least of these commandments and teaches men so shall be called least in the kingdom of heaven" (Mt 5:19). In the final commission to the disciples the Risen Lord commands them to go to all the nations (Mt 28:19), but in the mission charge of the tenth chapter the disciples are not to go among the Gentiles (Mt 10:5). The Pharisees are, on the one hand, hypocritical blind guides (Mt 23:13,16), but are, on the other hand, the ones who "sit on Moses' seat, so practice and observe whatever they tell you" (23:3). These are but a few of the interpretive dilemmas facing the reader of Matthew. The complex character of the material poses severe problems for the search for the work of the author. Because of these difficulties, there is a need for a critical key to the work of the redactor; a sure clue upon which further work can be anchored.[2]

One way to gain such a clue, in view of the proposed method, is to locate a passage or some passages where all three kinds of control over redaction analysis can be employed. Such a passage would have to contain: 1) a clear use of a source, 2) a definite logical pattern employed in the construction of

1. The need to understand Mt in the light of this complex material is now being recognized as a very important aspect in the definition of the situation of the author. K. Tagawa, in "People and Community in Matthew," 150, probes the question of the main purpose of Mt and says, "It is because of the fact that in Matthew there are contradictory ideas expressed side by side with no attempt at harmony that we ask such a hermeneutical question." Stendahl also, in the preface to the second edition of *The School of St. Matthew,* xiii, seeks to state a church situation in which the complexity of the gospel and its paradoxes could have existed. Their conclusions are very similar even though Stendahl stresses a Hellenistic milieu more than Tagawa does.

2. In view of the fact that none of the descriptive words available fully fit the work of the persons responsible for the final editions of our gospels, I think it best to use several terms to indicate this literary activity: redactor, writer, author, and editor. They are not simply editors, but are clearly not purely authors. They are not objective historians, but neither are they systematic theologians. Redactor is a helpful term because it is not familiar, but its basic meaning is an editor or reviser and that is not sufficient. Perhaps the work of these men lies beyond accurate label until we gain a much clearer picture of their work.

the passage and related to the source, and 3) elements of language, style, and motif which are also found in other portions of the gospel. Accordingly, the initial choice of a passage will be determined by the presence of the use of a source. If a passage can be found where a source has been used, then the investigation can proceed to the question of whether the passage yields a logical structure and also yields evidence of the literary traits of the redactor.[3]

The traditional approach to this initial choice has been to examine a passage where the use of Mark as a source can be detected. If there were certainty that Matthew used Mark, this would be a defensible procedure. But since Matthew's use of Mark is hypothetical, and since the use of this approach has thus far led to strikingly divergent views of the work of Matthew, another approach may be sought. The numerous references to the OT in Matthew provide another possible avenue of attack. If we should find that the citations and allusions to the OT have a direct relationship to the structure of the gospel, they will provide a key to the work of the writer.

There have been a number of studies concerning the citations in Matthew.[4] Stendahl's study of the formula citations in Matthew is of great help in determining the relationship of the citations to the OT text traditions, and it is also illuminating with regard to the Matthean understanding of the OT passages. Such a study is essential for an understanding of the meaning of the citations themselves. Yet, in important ways the work of Stendahl (and also Gundry)[5] concludes where the questions of redaction criticism are just emerging. That is to say, the examination of the relationship of the OT texts to their Matthean contexts is very limited. The attention paid to this subject concerns only the matter of how the texts are adapted to fit into Matthew.[6] As obvious and direct as this question is, it does not allow exploration of the wider and more subtle possibilities for the influence of the texts upon the structure of the passages around them.

Stendahl thinks that the variety in the character of the text of the OT citations that are peculiar to Matthew suggests that the gospel is the product

3. The use of an external source is not a necessary presupposition. If the author used none, then work must proceed without this control.

4. Among the many studies of the citations in Matthew the following may be noted: C. C. Torrey, "The Biblical Quotations in Matthew," in *Documents of the Primitive Church* (New York: Harper and Brothers, 1941), R. H. Gundry, *The Use of the Old Testament in St. Matthew's Gospel* and K. Stendahl, *The School of St. Matthew*. For a more extensive bibliography see the one provided by Stendahl, 42–43, in the footnotes.

5. The latter half of Gundry's work, 150–234, makes a number of sweeping judgments about Mt solely on the basis of this limited approach to the text form of the citations, and it is thus methodologically suspect.

6. The clearest example of this procedure is Stendahl's discussion of the Isaiah citation in Mt 12:18–21 (*School,* 108–115). Here the exact wording of the citation is shown to have been adapted to the preceding material by Matthew. In general, however, this is a topic tangential to Stendahl's work.

of a Christian scribal, exegetical school similar to that of Qumran.[7] In an article responding to Stendahl, B. Gärtner sought to show that the form of the text does not dictate a purely scribal or catechetical interest in the early church.[8] More important than the form of the text, according to Gärtner, is the milieu in early Christianity where such fulfilment citations were useful. That milieu was "the missionary preaching to the Jews."[9] If this is true, the use of the fulfilment texts is a part of a specific Christian apologetic. This insight leads to a question which, were the answer affirmative, would open an important door to an understanding of Matthew. Is it the case that the OT citations in Matthew are more than just proof-texting fulfilments? Are there instances in which a theological understanding related to the cited text provides the structure for what precedes the text, or what follows it, or both? The analyses in this chapter explore these questions in relation to some of the citations of and allusion to the OT in Matthew.

In order to maintain the focus of this study on the problems of Matthean redaction, the discussion of the effects of the analyses upon source and form critical questions will be limited to those instances which are in my judgment of major importance. However, this is a limitation determined by practical necessity and not by method. At every point these and any other redaction analyses must be considered a part of the entire exegetical enterprise.

ANALYSIS 1: MT 13:1–52

The great parables discourse of Mt 13 contains a number of features which make it an excellent choice for an initial test of the method and of the working hypothesis. Within its 52 verses are sections which can readily be identified as traditions which have been taken up by the author—namely, the parables. There are also two important references to the OT: Isa 6:9–10 in the section 13:13–17 and Ps 78:2 in 13:35.[10] Moreover, the structure of the discourse has long presented a problem for interpreters.[11] Thus, the section is one where redaction analysis is very important, and it contains the OT

7. Stendahl, *School,* 20–35.

8. "The Habakkuk Commentary and the Gospel of Matthew," *ST* 8 (1954) 1–24. Especially important are pp. 22–24.

9. Gärtner, 23.

10. Other allusions to the OT occur in the chapter but as integral parts of sentences and phrases: Zeph 1:3 is alluded to in vs. 41, and the reference to the "birds of the heavens" in the Mustard Seed parable is a familiar OT phrase (Ps 104:12 *et al.*).

11. In addition to the work of scholars who investigate the parables as a group, there have been recent special studies of this chapter: J. Gnilka, *Die Verstockung Israels,* (München: Kösel-Verlag, 1961), W. Wilkens, "Die Redaction des Gleichniskapitels Mark. 4 durch Matth.," *TZ* 20 (1964) 305–327, and J. D. Kingsbury, *The Parables of Jesus in Matthew 13* (London: SPCK, 1969).

elements that are necessary for a testing of the hypothesis that Matthew has shaped parts of his gospel by conscious use of the OT citations.

The chapter may be outlined as follows:

1–3a Introduction
3b–9 The parable of the Sower
10–17 The theory of the parables
14–15 Isa 6:9–10 LXX
18–23 The interpretation of the Sower
24–30 The parable of the Tares
31–32 The parable of the Mustard Seed
33 The parable of the Leaven
34 A summary concerning parabolic teaching
35 A formula citation: Ps 78:2
36–43 The interpretation of the Tares
44 The parable of the Treasure
45–46 The parable of the Pearl
47–48 The parable of the Net
49–50 The interpretation of the Net
51–52 A conclusion concerning the disciples' comprehension and the work of a "scribe trained for the kingdom of heaven."

A preliminary form-critical analysis reveals that the chapter is made up of the following elements. There are seven parables, six of which are kingdom parables. The six kingdom parables comprise three sets of twin parables. That is, they are pairs of parables which use different images to make the same point.[12] They are: Mustard Seed and Leaven, Treasure and Pearl, and Net and Tares. The Sower parable is neither a twin nor a kingdom parable. Three of the seven parables are interpreted: Sower, Tares, and Net. All three interpretations deal with the separation of persons demanded by the requirements for participation in the kingdom of heaven. There are two major OT references. Isa 6:9 is alluded to in vs. 13 and quoted fully in vss. 14–15. Ps 78:2 appears in vs. 35 as a standard Matthean formula quotation.[13] Woven among these blocks of material are three transitional passages which treat the subject of the correct use of the parables: vss. 10–13 and 16–17, vs 34, and vss. 51–52. These are the building blocks from which the chapter is constructed.

12. J. Jeremias, *The Parables of Jesus*, 90–92, discusses twin parables. He says, "We find in the first three gospels a great number of paired parables and similes where the same ideas are expressed in different symbols." This feature of the parables in Mt 13 will be very important as the analysis proceeds.

13. Using this term as it has been defined by Sherman Johnson, "The Biblical Quotations in Matthew," *HTR* 36 (1943) 135ff., and taken up by Stendahl and Gundry.

A LINEAR READING OF 13:1–52

The introductory verses provide the setting for the chapter. A crowd gathers and Jesus teaches them in parables (13:1–3a). A comparison of these verses with 5:1f., 10:1f., 18:1f., 23:1, and 24:1 shows that Matthew has no stereotyped formula for beginning a discourse.

However, the parallels between 5:1–2 and 13:1–3a are striking. Jesus is seated (κάθημαι) in a special place (5:1 on a mountain // 13:2 in a boat on the shore) and the crowds (ὄχλοι) are gathered around him (5:1 // 13:2). In 5:1–2 and 23:1 both the crowds and the disciples are gathered. In 10:1, 18:1, and 24:1 only the disciples are addressed. Two suggestions may be drawn from these comparisons. First, the similarities between the setting for the Sermon on the Mount and the Parables Discourse suggest that the settings are the work of the same person. Even if here he utilizes a source, such as Mark, the author has still shaped the verses so that they parallel the opening of the Sermon on the Mount in a way that Mk 4:1 does not. And second, the audience of each of the discourses is consistently adapted to the content of the discourse.[14] The latter suggestion will prove important in following the structure of the parables discourse.

The situation is quite different in the case of the parable of the Sower. A source has very likely been employed for the parable. There is no evidence of redactional modification of a simple and straightforward narrative account. The major problem for an understanding of the Sower in the discourse is the choice of this particular parable. It is unique among the parables of the chapter in not being a kingdom parable. Why should this non-kingdom parable introduce a discourse so largely devoted to the kingdom parables and the relationship between the parables and the kingdom? Two answers seem possible. The Sower may have stood at this point in a source which the author is following, or this parable may have been considered a very popular example of Jesus' parables and therefore an appropriate one for the beginning of a discourse made up of parables and their interpretations.[15] Further evidence about the composition of the chapter is necessary before this question can be dealt with adequately.

The conclusion to the parable of the Sower as it stands in Matthew is a cryptic command, "He who has ears, let him hear!" Although most commentators have considered these words to be simply an addition made at some stage in the tradition exhorting the hearers to seriousness,[16] the phrase

14. The importance of the audience in this discourse has been widely noted. See especially the article by Wilkens, "Die Redaction des Gleischniskapitels Mark. 4 durch Matth."

15. The natural assumption, given the present state of criticism, is that the source was Mark. However, honoring the principle of independent linear reading, judgment is withheld. Actually, the problem of the choice of the Sower is important for Marcan studies as well.

16. Jeremias, *The Parables of Jesus,* 109–110.

may be an exegetical formula. This prhase is used in Jewish literature to call for assent to the exegetical comment (*Mekilta* 19:5, *Sifre Lev.* 7:18, *et al.*). The other occurrences in Matthew (11:15 and 13:32) appear in close conjunction with OT citations. Even Rev 13:9, though less clear, may depend upon such a use of the formula. B. Gerhardsson has recently argued that the Sower is clearly reminiscent of the *Shema* and is intended to be a comment upon it.[17] If so, at some point in the transmission of the Sower, the formula was attached to it. This could have been done by Jesus himself or at some point along the way before Matthew. There is good reason to believe that it was not done by Matthew. Matthew uses the formula in connection with direct citations and their interpretation in 11:15 and 13:43. Moreover, nothing in the interpretation of the Sower or theory of parable in Matthew suggests that Matthew perceives an exegesis within the parable itself.

The formula in vs. 9 is of great importance to Matthew, however, because it suggests that one ought to be able to understand the meaning of the parable of the Sower. That sets the stage for the query of the disciples, "Why do you speak to them in parables?" In other words, why not speak directly instead of in parables? Through the call to hearing and the question of the disciples, the issue around which the rest of the chapter will turn, "What is the purpose of the parables?" is raised.

An initial answer to the disciples' question is given in vss. 11–12.

> Because[18]
> it has been given to you to know the secrets of the kingdom of heaven.
> But to them it has not been given.
> For whoever has will be given more,
> and whoever has nothing will have even that taken from him.

It has often been maintained that Matthew combines these couplets solely on the basis of the catchword *give*. That suggestion misses the point of the passage. Instead of catchword, a theory of exegesis and of eschatology is involved. The key concept in the theory is "to you it has been given to know the secrets of the kingdom of heaven."

What have Jesus' parables to do with this cryptic language? To find an answer, the meaning of the term *secrets* in early Jewish literature must be recalled. The term was a commonplace one in apocalyptic literature. A close parallel to the use of the concept of secrets in Mt 13 is to be found in the Qumran writings.[19]

17. B. Gerhardsson, "The Parable of the Sower and its Interpretation," *NTS* 14 (1968) 165–193. Though he is unaware of the use of this formula in Jewish literature to conclude an exegesis, the evidence about the formula would strengthen his argument.

18. That the ὅτι here is intentionally causal is demonstrated in the rest of the analysis. However, the causal nature of the clauses has also been seen by D. O. Via in "Matthew on the Understandability of the Parables," *JBL* 84 (1965) 430–432.

19. An excellent treatment of the idea of secrets at Qumran in relation to their exegesis is given by O. Betz, *Offenbarung und Schriftforschung in der Qumransekte,* (Tübingen: J. C. B.

The general concept of divine revelation at Qumran was built upon the belief that God had hidden his plan for history and his will for men in the Torah and the Prophets. Their covenant—

> a binding oath to return with all his heart and soul to the commandments of the Law of Moses, as that Law is revealed to the sons of Zadok—that is, to the priests who still keep the Covenant and keep God's will (1QS 5:8f.).[20]

The OT text in and of itself is not revelation until it is interpreted correctly by one who has been instructed by the Holy Spirit (1QH 12:11f.).[21]

Within this overall picture of revelation the prophets held special significance. The prophets were believed to have delivered messages which were intended for the men of the end time and could not be understood even by the prophets themselves.

> God told Habakkuk to write down the things that were to come upon the latter age, but He did not inform him when that moment would come to fulfillment. As to the phrase, "that he who runs may read," this refers to the teacher who expounds the Law aright, for God has made him "au courant" with all the deeper implications (רזי) of the words of his servants the prophets. (1QpHab 7:1ff.).

The secrets were open only to the Teacher who was properly trained to read the text. Those Outside had no access to the secrets even though they possessed the sacred texts.[21a]

The content of the secrets was quite specific. They were "the things that were to come upon the latter age." The message of the prophets was for the Qumran community a storehouse of the eschatological secrets which could only be brought to light by God through a properly trained interpreter.

The parallel between this view of the Scriptures and Matthew's understanding of the meaning of the parables of Jesus is precise. According to both, the plan and will of God are given in publicly available teachings but they can only be perceived by the special few. To the others the secrets remain hidden.[22] According to both, the knowledge of the secrets is knowledge of the impending judgment. At that judgment the ones who know

---

Mohr, 1960), esp. 73–78. R. E. Brown, *The Semitic Background of the Term "Mystery" in the New Testament* (Philadelphia: Fortress Press, 1968), has largely missed the parallel use of secrets in Mt 13 and in Qumran.

20. Eng. tr. that of T. H. Gaster, *The Dead Sea Scriptures* (New York: Doubleday & Co., Inc., 1956), but the citations follow the more common method of column and line.

21. Betz, *Offenbarung*, 119ff.

21a. The fact that others comprehend the meaning of the parables, as the chief priest and Pharisees do in 12:45, does not contradict Matthew's theory, as Kingsbury claims in *The Parables of Jesus in Matthew 13*, 49–50, because those outside lack the secrets which would compel their acceptance (or, "understanding," in Mt's sense) of the message.

22. Though scholars have sensed that the parables were not told to veil secrets from the public, they have not grasped the special concepts which underlie the theory of parable as it appears in the gospels. Jeremias, *The Parables*, 15–19, attempts to argue that the theory originally did not refer to parables.

the secrets will be blessed and the outsiders will be punished. Thus Mt 13:11–12 expresses ideas consistent with those found in the Habakkuk Pesher. But the materials which hold the secrets are very different. For Qumran they are the Prophets and the Torah, while for Matthew they are the parables of Jesus.

A second and correlative answer to the question of the purpose of the parables is provided in vss. 13–17. Before that answer can be fully treated, the problem regarding the authenticity in Matthew of the full quotation of Isa 6:9–10, which appears in Mt 13:14–15, must be considered.

Stendahl and Gnilka have held that the full citation of the Isaiah text is an early interpolation into Matthew under the influence of its use in Acts 28:26ff.[23] Stendahl gives the following reasons for this view. 1) Of all the formula citations in Matthew, this is the only one which Jesus himself utters. 2) This text and the even more suspect text in Mt 12:40 are the only texts in Matthew which conform completely to the Septuagint. 3) The introductory formula uses two key words which are found nowhere else in Matthew's rather stereotyped introductions: ἀναπληροῦται and προφητεία.[24] Also, the text interrupts the sense of the construction of vss. 13, 16–17. Against the assumption of an interpolation stands all of the textual evidence.[25] And it is not beyond the realm of possibility that the author, realizing how heavily his theory in vss. 13 and 16–17 depended upon the Isa 6:9–10 text, felt it important to include the full citation. The unique situation presented by placing the citation on Jesus' lips might have occasioned the altered formula. On balance I find the evidence against the citation's genuine place in Matthew far stronger than the arguments for it. It will not be dealt with in the rest of this analysis. It should be added, however, that it may be genuine, but this would not materially affect the analysis. The line of the author's thought is to be discerned in his use of the allusions to Isa 6:9–10, whether or not the full text was actually cited.

In vss. 13, 16–17, there is a careful allusion to Isa 6:9–10. The intricate relationship between the Matthean verses and the Isaiah text may be illustrated by italicizing the important words.

(Matthew)	(Isaiah)
13 Because they *look* but do not *see* and *hear* but do not *hear*. nor do they *understand*.	9 *Hear* and *hear*, but do not *understand;* *see* and *see*, but do not perceive.
16 But blessed are your *eyes* because they *see*	10 Make the heart of this people fat, and their *ears* heavy,

23. Stendahl, *School*, 129ff., and Gnilka, *Die Verstockung*, 103–105.

24. Stendahl, *School*, 130–131.

25. But Stendahl does note that only in this text does cod. D sharply diverge from the other manuscripts in a Matthean OT citation (*School*, 131).

And your *ears*
because they *hear*.

17 I tell you,
many prophets and righteous men
longed to *see* what you *see*,
and *hear* what you *hear*,
But they did not *hear*.

and shut their *eyes*,
Lest they *see* with their *eyes*,
and *hear* with their *ears*,
And *understand* with their hearts,
and turn and be healed.

Through his use of these verses, a connection is drawn between the theory of parables stated in vss. 11–12 and the interpretation of the Sower. This can be seen in a study of the pronouns in the texts written above. In Isaiah all the people fail to *see* and *hear* and *understand.* There is no contrast. But in Matthew the stress upon the emphatic second person plural pronoun in vss. 16–17 draws the contrast between the ones who do not see or hear and understand in vs. 13 (along with the prophets and righteous men in vs. 17) and *you,* the disciples, who do *see* and *hear*.

The meaning of vss. 13–17 is parallel to the initial answer to the disciples' question. The crowds are given the parables. But they are unable to grasp their meaning. They fail to grasp the secrets. The disciples, on the other hand, are also given the parables, but because it has been given to them to know the secrets, they can see and hear and understand. Not even the prophets and righteous men of old were so privileged. Here, as elsewhere in Matthew, to be blessed means to be guaranteed participation in the Kingdom of Heaven (cf. the Beatitudes in 5:1–12 and the Judgment picture in 25:31–46).[26] From Isa 6:9–10 just those elements have been drawn which reinforce the theory of parables and they are woven into a virtual restatement of that theory. It has firmly underlined hearing and understanding. There is no interest, as in Mark, in the hardening of the hearts portion of the text, but only concentration in single-minded fashion upon the secrets theory of parable interpretation.

The parable of the Sower had concluded in vs. 9 with the call to hear. Matthew now returns to that theme in introducing an interpretation of that parable: "You [the disciples] hear the parable of the Sower!" If Matthew is working as carefully as it now appears, some effect of the theory of parables should appear in the interpretation of the Sower. That effect is now readily seen in the use of the terms hear and understand, and in identifying the seed as "the word of the Kingdom."

26. H. J. Held, in "On the Essence of Being a Disciple," *Tradition and Interpretation in Matthew,* 107, treats the sequence of ideas in vss. 13, 16 and 17 as logically related to vs. 11, but he does not mention the allusions to the Isa text, and he understands "secrets" in vs. 12 as "doctrines" (footnote 3) and later makes this equal "the Christian message as a whole" (109). By such an interpretation Held changes the eschatological terminology of the passage into catechetical terminology. The difference between Held's view and Matthew's intentions can be seen in the emphasis upon the kingdom and separation of good from evil in the rest of the discourse.

Everyone who *hears* the *word of the Kingdom* and does not *understand* . . . , vs. 19.
This is the one who *hears* the word and immediately accepts it . . . , vs. 20.
This is the one who *hears* the word and the cares of the world . . . , vs. 22.
This is the one who *hears* and *understands* and bears fruit . . . , vs. 23.

Not one of the italicized elements, those elements which carry the meaning of the interpretation, comes from the parable itself. But all of these terms except *word* (λόγος) do occur in the theory of parables section (*hear* in vss. 13, 16, 17; *kingdom* in vs. 11; and *understand* in vs. 15). The contrast drawn in the Matthean form of the interpretation of the sower is not among four kinds of people but only between two kinds—those who *hear and understand* (vs. 23) and those who *hear* but *do not understand* (vss. 19, 20, 22).[27] There can be little doubt that the interpretation of the Sower in Matthew is constructed on the model of the theory for interpreting the parables of vss. 11–17 and that this has been done through the use of the key words *kingdom, hear* and *understand.*[28]

In his effort to interpret this parable according to the theory of parables Matthew encounters some difficulty. A non-kingdom parable must be made one by allegory.[28a] In the process soils and seeds are necessarily confused (cf. vs. 19 with vs. 29). This confusion in the imagery of the interpretation is further evidence that the line of interpretation is foreign to the parable itself and derives instead from the theory of parables. Matthew has linked together the parable of the Sower, his theory of parables, and the interpretation of the Sower by means of careful use of the allusions to Isa 6:9–10. This method of linking materials by means of the OT may be termed mid-point construction.

Matthew has now been able to develop a theory of interpretation of the parables of Jesus which coincides closely with the theory of pesher interpretation of the Prophets at Qumran. According to this theory, the parables contain within them "secrets" concerning the end-time. These secrets are not open to the casual listener or reader but can only be grasped by the ones

27. Gerhardsson may be right that the use of the phrases *ἐν τῇ καρδίᾳ* vs. 19, *ἐν ἑαυτῷ* vs. 21 and *ἡ μέριμνα τοῦ αἰῶνος* in vs. 22 for the poor soils reflects Jewish exegesis of the *Shema,* but the weight of the interpretation still falls on the allusions to the words of Isa 6:9, "hear and understand."

28. This must be said of the Matthean form no matter what decision is made on the Synoptic relationships. The emphasis in both the Marcan and Lucan forms is on the term *word* (Mk 4:14, 15,16,18,19,20 and Lk 8:11,12,13,15), and no connections are drawn to the theory of parables. Kingsbury, *The Parables of Jesus In Matthew 13,* 54, recognizes that this use of catchword means that "the Interpretation of the Parable of the Sower is thus firmly bound to the Reason for Speaking in Parables."

28a. When Kingsbury says, "Still, the very presence of this story of the Sower in Matthew's parable chapter marks it as a 'parable of the Kingdom,'" in *The Parables of Jesus in Matthew 13,* 33, he arbitrarily allows Matthew's view of the parable to determine its original meaning.

privileged to know the secrets, that is, the disciples. Moreover, the theory has been applied to one of Jesus' parables, the Sower.

The next element in the discourse is the parable of the Tares. It has long been something of a riddle to interpreters. What led Matthew to choose this parable? The thread which has now developed in the construction allows us to answer that question with a measure of confidence. In vs. 3 the statement is made explicitly that the teaching involved was of many parables. In the first 23 verses of the discourse Matthew has presented a parable of *sowing* in connection with a theory of parable interpretation which stresses the revelation of the *secrets* of the *kingdom of heaven.* Then he has interpreted the Sower as a *kingdom* parable dealing with the *separation* of those who perceive the secrets from those who do not. The author now turns to a *kingdom* parable about *sowing* which stresses *separation,* the parable of the Tares. There can now be little doubt that the choice of this parable is dictated by the flow of thought which has developed in the preceding verses.

The parable of the Tares is told in straightforward fashion. Little more than the introductory phrase, "He taught them another parable, saying . . . ," could be assigned to the author. Perhaps also he has written *kingdom of heaven* for a simpler *kingdom* or even *kingdom of God* since this phrase is clearly a favorite of his (33 times in the gospel). The bulk of the parable gives evidence of being from a source or oral tradition available to Matthew.

Tares is followed in Matthew by the twin parables of Mustard Seed and Leaven.[29] The same introductory phrase is used as that for the Tares and no logical link is provided. They are, like Tares, kingdom parables which begin with the phrase, "The kingdom of heaven is like. . . ." In all likelihood then, Matthew has selected Tares from a source containing kingdom parables and has simply gone on giving parables from that source as some of the "many parables" that Jesus taught. By now it is apparent that, although Matthew has been less than careful in identifying the audience (13:24 does not make clear that the *αὐτοῖς* is the crowd and not the disciples), the parables are directed to the *original crowd* (vs. 2), while the answer to the disciples' question and the interpretation of the Sower were addressed only to the disciples.

After the parable of the Leaven, a verse appears which looks like a conclusion to the series even though there is a great deal of the discourse remaining. "All these things Jesus spoke to the crowds in parables, and apart from parables he did not teach them anything" (vs. 34). While there is little in this verse to give clues to redaction, it should be noted that the last phrase conforms to the theory of parables. That is, it asserts that Jesus only taught the crowds in the form of parables which veil the *secrets.*

This verse is closely followed by a citation text which appears at first

29. A fine treatment of these two parables is that by J. Dupont, "Les paraboles du sénevé et du levain," *NRT* 89 (1967) 897–913.

glance to be a direct contradiction of the intent of the summary in vs. 34. The quotation is Ps 78:2:

> I will open my mouth in parables;
> I will reveal secrets hidden from the foundation of the world.

The psalmist is speaking of an open revelation, as is made clear by the next verses:

> things that we have heard and known,
>   that our fathers have told us.
> We will not hide them from their children,
>   but tell to the coming generation
>   the glorious deeds of the Lord. . . . (Ps 78:3–4).

But just as he was not bound by Isaiah's intention in shaping his use of Isa 6:9–10, so Matthew is not bound by the psalmist's intention. Instead, he reads the verse as a direct confirmation of his theory of parables. That is, Jesus has opened his mouth in parables and in them he has revealed the secrets of the endtime which have been hidden from the foundation of the world.[30] In view of the parables theory, Matthew means that the parables reveal the secret hidden things only to the disciples. Therefore, it is possible that the last phrase of vs. 34 reflects Matthew's work, and it is clear that the citation is governed by Matthew's theory. The textual evidence helps to confirm this. The first line of the citation conforms closely with the LXX, especially in reading the plural "parables." The second half is just as clearly dependent on the Hebrew in speaking of "hidden things" and "from the foundation."[31]

In this text from the Psalms the author found important confirmation for his Qumran-like understanding of the meaning of the parables. Accordingly he is now prompted to give another example of the interpretation of a parable so that he can show how the "hidden things" are revealed in the parables.[32] Of the three preceding parables (Tares, Mustard Seed, Leaven) only Tares combines the kingdom and the separation motifs. So it is the one to receive interpretation. Once again the OT passage has served as a middle term in the construction of the discourse. The role of the citation as a middle term provides the only adequate explanation for the separation of the parable of the Tares from its interpretation.

The parable of the Tares suits Matthew's theory of the parables far better than the Sower did. In the Sower the allegory was imprecise, but in the Tares the correspondences may be exact. The one who sows the good seed is the

30. For the standard apocalyptic connection between creation and end time see Betz, *Offenbarung*, 83–84.

31. On the peculiarities of the Matthean citation see Stendahl, *School*, 116–117.

32. W. Wilkens, "Die Redaktion des Gleichniskapitels Mark. 4 durch Matth. 13." 320–321, correctly grasps the fact that vss. 34–35 are transitional in Mt but fails to perceive the nature of the transition which is made in Mt in accord with the theory in vss. 10–17.

Son of Man (vs. 37). The field is the world (vs. 38). The good seed are the sons of the kingdom (vs. 38). The tares are the sons of the evil one (vs. 38). The one who sowed them is the devil (vs. 39). The harvest is the judgment (vs. 39). The harvesters are the angels (vs. 39). Throughout the passage the signs of Matthean authorship are unmistakable: "sons of the evil one," "the close of the age," and "the sons of the kingdom."[33] Matthew carefully establishes the equations and then shows how the action of the parable relates to the end-time in vss. 40–43. At that time the kingdom (field/world) will be purged of the evildoers and the kingdom will be established.[34] In Matthew's pesher interpretation of the parables, the same rigid dualism is in effect as in the theology of Qumran; the sons of the kingdom struggle against the sons of the evil one.[35] The interpretation of the Tares is a very clear example of Matthew's method of interpreting the parables.[36]

The Matthean interpretation of the Tares is one of the passages where some scholars have found evidence of a double front in the gospel.[37] The theory is that at several points in the gospel the author is concerned to deal with external opposition to God's will and with intra-church apostasy in successive passages. Advocates of this position hold that in vs. 41 the statement that "the angels of the Son of Man will gather out of his kingdom all those who stumble and are doers of lawlessness," indicates a struggle within the church between Matthew's more orthodox party and a libertine group. The theory may be defensible elsewhere in the gospel, but it can be supported in this verse only if it is wrenched out of context.[38] In its Matthean context the imagery is clearly directed against one group of evil

33. Jeremias has collected no fewer than 37 Matthean characteristics in the 8 verses (*The Parables,* 83–85).

34. This means that the kingdom of the Son of Man (vs. 41), from which the weeds/evildoers are evicted, is ultimately the kingdom of their Father (vs. 43). There is no hint in the interpretation that any other arena of separation exists than this arena of field-world-kingdom. The ambiguity between the kingdom of the Son of Man and that of the Father is not unique here. It is also present in 25:34, "Then the King will say to those at his right hand, 'Come, O blessed of my Father, inherit the kingdom prepared for you from the foundation of the world.'" Apparently the Father's kingdom is only fulfilled when the Son of Man has purged the world of evil ones.

35. The similarity of perspective to the "War of the Sons of Light against the Sons of Darkness" is readily apparent. This is not confined to Qumran attitude, however, for it is widely attested in Jewish apocalyptic.

36. That Matthew intends it to be understood as an interpretation is shown by his use of the exegetical formula, "He who has ears, let him hear" (vs. 43). Moreover, this shows that for Matthew an exegesis of a parable requires the same kind of assent as exegesis of an OT text because here he expects the reader to grasp both the interpretation of the parable and the fact that it has revealed the "things hidden from the foundation" of Ps 78:2.

37. Among those who speak of the double front are Bornkamm, Trilling, and Strecker. In *Tradition and Interpretation,* 19ff., Bornkamm gives a clear statement of the position.

38. Strecker, *Der Weg,* 218, separates vss. 36–39 from 40–43. He holds the former to have been tradition, the latter to be Matthean double front interpretation. The claim defies the literary data gathered by Jeremias as well as the logical data adduced here.

ones sown into the world by the devil. The perspective is far wider than the church. The world is a neutral term in vs. 38. The Son of Man will take full domain over the cosmos, his kingdom, by expelling the intruding sons of the evil one. The advocates of the double front miss this point and think that those who stumble and are doers of lawlessness are among the sons of the kingdom. Both groups are in the same field, the world, but they are not one community. The interpretation is a simple dualistic one in which the conflict of good and evil is resolved in the judgment by the victory of the Son of Man, his angels, and sons of the kingdom (vs. 43).[38a]

Three more kingdom parables follow the interpretation of the Tares: Treasure, Pearl, and Net. The first is given no introduction whatever; the last two are introduced simply by "again." They are all kingdom parables, are all introduced by the phrase "the kingdom is like," and all appear to be from the same source as Tares, Mustard Seed, and Leaven (see below for further discussion of the series of twin parables as a source).

The interpretation of the parable of the Net in vss. 49–50 is a parallel to the earlier interpretation of the Tares. The similarity of language in the two interpretations makes it clear that they are both of Matthean origin and are to be understood in the same way.[39] This parallel in the interpretations is hardly surprising because the parables are another set of twins. The net is cast into the sea. As the plants in the field were mixed between the good plants and the tares, so the fish in the sea are mixed. The net brings up a portion of this mixture. The good are separated from the bad. Advocates of the double front erroneously identify the net with the church, but just as a field is only a part of the land world, so the part of the sea enclosed by a net is just a part of the sea and can be a figure for the whole sea. The imagery is still consistently dualistic and has no reference to an inner-church conflict.[40]

The interpretation of the parable of the Net, which parallels so closely the interpretation of the Tares, links the last series of parables (Treasure, Pearl,

38a. The precise use of the imagery from the parable and the clear application of the Matthean theory in the interpretation renders Kingsbury's judgment, *The Parables of Jesus in Matthew 13,* 66, that "the Interpretation of the Parable of the Tares is only apparently, not really, an explanation of the parable of the Tares," very difficult to defend. What would be required for it to be "really" such an interpretation?

39. Some of the parallels are:

vs. 40 and 49: οὕτως ἔσται ἐν τῇ συντελείᾳ
vss. 42 and 50: ἐκεῖ ἔσται ὁ κλαυθμὸς καὶ ὁ βρυγμὸς τῶν ὀδόντων

See Jeremias, *The Parables of Jesus,* 85.

40. The failure of J. D. Kingsbury to see the fact that Net and Tares are twin parables produces the most serious disruption of his logic, and he therefore forces the material of the chapter into other patterns alien to it (*The Parables of Jesus in Matthew 13,* 14 and 117f.). Kingsbury's error is similar to Strecker's. The parables are visual images, not primarily literary, and neither writer has paused to visualize the situation of a fisherman casting his net into the sea.

and Net) to the rest of the chapter. It does so not only by the parallelism of the interpretation of the Tares and the Net, but also by providing a final application of the parables theory. For Matthew the interpretation of the Net shows once more how the parables of Jesus contain the secrets of the coming kingdom of heaven.

The conclusion of the discourse in vss. 51–52 summarizes both the content and the purpose of the chapter. The original audience, the crowd, has been left behind since the introduction to the interpretation of the Tares (vs. 36). It is by now clear that the crowds are only incidental to Matthew's purpose. The purpose of the discourse has been reached through putting the parables theory and the interpretation of three parables into a setting in which Jesus is instructing the disciples. Now Jesus asks,

> "Have you understood all this?" They said to him, "Yes." And he said to them, "Therefore every scribe who has been trained for the kingdom of heaven is like a householder who brings out of his treasure what is new and what is old."

This conclusion has important implications. The disciples are the ones to whom it has been given to know the secrets of the kingdom of heaven, and now they know what that means. In Matthew's parables discourse the disciples are not obtuse. They respond favorably to Jesus' instruction. A disciple trained for the kingdom of heaven is now able to see the eschatological theory of interpretation by which he can unlock the secrets of the coming judgment that are "hidden" from the public in the parables of Jesus. There may be double meaning in the words "old things and new things." The Christian scribe will bring forth new things; i.e., secrets of the end-time, and old things, i.e., things hidden since creation. Moreoever the Christian scribe has in his storehouse not just the texts of the OT but also the parables of Jesus as resources for discovering the secrets. He holds the key to the secrets. That key is the eschatological exegesis espoused by Matthew and supported by the careful use of the suitable OT texts, Isa 6:9-10 and Ps 78:2.[40a]

The tracing of Matthew's thought through the discourse has been completed. The discovery of the pivotal roles of the OT texts and the special theory of parable interpretation has led to an unraveling of a number of exegetical problems in the chapter. However, two residual problems need attention.

First the suggestion has been strong that Matthew is utilizing a kingdom parables source for the six kingdom parables in the chapter. It is now possible to gather the evidence and assess it. There are three sets of twin parables. They all begin with a phrase comparing something or some act to the kingdom. But one of the sets, Tares and Net, is separated whereas the

40a. Kingsbury, *The Parables of Jesus in Matthew 13,* 125–129, notes the link between vs. 51 and vs. 36 but fails to see that "understand all these things" also recalls the theory of parables in 13:10–17 (esp. the key word, "understand") and that vss. 51–52 provide a conclusion to the entire discourse rather than just to the material in vss. 36–50.

other two sets appear together. Furthermore, a seemingly unnecessary conclusion appears in the midst of the kingdom parables, vs. 34. All of this leads me to suggest that the author did in fact have a source containing kingdom parables that were paired parables and that the order of that source can be partially reconstructed from the data in Mt 13.

The reconstruction would be:

Treasure
Pearl
Net
——→
Tares
Mustard Seed
Leaven
Conclusion (vs. 34)

Matthew selected the parable of the Tares as the one most appropriate to follow the Sower, the theory of parables, and the interpretation of the Sower. He did so because only Tares combined the elements of the kingdom, sowing, and separation. By selecting the parable of the Tares, Matthew interrupted the series of twin kingdom parables between Net and Tares (see arrow in outline above). When he reached the conclusion of the source, he may have copied it:

"All this Jesus said to the crowds in parables" (34). But in order to make it conform to his theory of parables it is quite likely that he added:

"Indeed he said nothing to them without a parable" (34b).

Taking the "speaking in parables" as a direct confirmation of the first half of Ps 78:2, he introduced that text as a formula citation. Then, because the second half of the verse opened up once more the subject of the secrets or hidden things, Matthew went on to interpret the parable of the Tares. He then included the rest of, or some of, the parables which preceded Tares in the source and rounded off the section with the interpretation of the Net. (Net must have preceded Tares, see arrow in reconstruction above.) The result was a parables discourse consisting primarily of kingdom parables arranged in this curious order. The two keys which allow the reconstruction of the source are the separation of the twin parables Net and Tares, and the presence within the discourse of the conclusion to the kingdom parables source.

Did Matthew use all of the source in chapter 13? This is a difficult question. Since no formal introduction that might indicate the beginning of a source is given to the parable of the Treasure, Matthew may have selected only some of the parables from the source. Are there other Synoptic parables which might have belonged to the source? The requirements for their identification would be: 1) they would have to be kingdom parables, 2) they would have to be introduced by the comparative phrase, and 3) they would need to be twin parables. Without all three items of evidence, no claim could be made for inclusion in the source. There are four other Matthean parables which qualify on requirements 1) and 2) The Unforgiving Servant, 18:21–35, The Workers in the Vineyard, 20:1-16, The Marriage Feast, 22:1–14, and The Wise and Foolish Virgins, 25:1–13. However, none of them are twin parables, and they are too long for anyone to suspect that they might ever have been twins. It seems likely that, while we cannot say whether Matthew has used all of his source, no other portions of the source are now recoverable. Moreoever, Matthew appears to have been so fond of the introductory phrase from the source that he freely used it with other parables to which it may not have been original.[41]

The other remaining problem is the presence of the Sower in a discourse so dominated by kingdom parables and a kingdom theory of interpretation. It has been suggested (above, p. 15) that there are two ways of explaining the use of the parable of the Sower. It may have stood in a source used by the author, or it may have been considered a fine example of the parables and the natural one with which to begin a discourse on the parables.

There does not appear to be any way of answering this question from the evidence in Matthew. Since the opening verses of the discourse have been at least partially shaped by Matthew, the use of a source is not certainly established. And since no rationale for the choice of the parable of the Sower has been discovered in the analysis, the reason for the choice can only be surmised if a source is not the answer. As a result, further discussion of this question must be taken up in the light of the Synoptic relationships. The redactional evidence is inconclusive.

Although some of the steps of the linear analysis are thus tentative, the overall portrait of Matthew's work in the chapter has been drawn. From13:10 to 13:52 the hand of the author has been traced as he shaped and combined and created the materials which make up the analysis. It is now necessary to assess the results of the linear analysis.

THE ANALYSIS AND THE CONTROLS

Mt 13:1–52 has been examined by means of linear analysis. It is now important to assess the degree of certainty which can be claimed for the position that it was the author of Matthew who gave the discourse the shape that has been outlined.

41. The comparison phrase is appropriate for the Great Supper parable (22:1–14) but somewhat less appropriate for the Unforgiving Servant (18:23-35), the Laborers in the Vineyard (20:1–16), and the Ten Virgins (25:1–13). Kingsbury accurately concludes that the use of this phrase "is thoroughly indicative of the milieu of the first Gospel" (*The Parables of Jesus in Matthew 13,* 20).

Because this is the first analysis, only limited use has been made of the third type of control, Matthean characteristics of style, vocabulary, and motif. However, there have been points at which such evidence has been important. The emphasis on kingdom of heaven has reflected the author's favorite way of speaking of the kingdom. More importantly, the presence in the interpretation of the Tares and of the Net of characteristic Matthean phrases has been used to identify these portions as the work of the redactor (above, pp. 23, 24, 25). The control has also been important in a negative way. The absence of Matthean characteristics in the seven parables has helped, along with other more positive indications, to show that these have been taken over from tradition by the author.

Application of the first type of redactional control, that is, a clearly discernible logical thread, has been far more important for this analysis than Matthean characteristics. Its value must be assessed in conjunction with the other type of control, the use of the OT as a source. It has been shown that Matthew employs a distinctive theory of the meaning of Jesus' parables as the controlling feature of the discourse. The theory of interpreting the parables is so closely parallel to the Qumran theory of interpreting the Prophets that the evidence from the Habakkuk Commentary has been helpful in tracing the ideas of Matthew. And in the shaping of the theory of parables, the interpretation of the Sower, and the interpretation of the Tares, the author has used two OT passages, Isa 6:9–10 and Ps 78:2. He has, however, shown considerable freedom in using the OT passage to suit his purposes. This freedom can be seen by contrasting the meaning of the OT texts in their contexts with their meaning in the Matthean context. In this way the second type of control, the use of a source, is closely related to the logical structure of the passage. The result of this convergence of controls has been that exact literary evidence can be marshalled to demonstrate the line of the author's thought. An example is the use by the author of the words of Isa 6:9–10 to shape the interpretation of the Sower (above, pp. 19–21). Adding strength to the analysis is the fact that virtually none of the material falls outside the scope of the discovered redactional organization. On the basis of the controls, therefore, it is highly probable that the redactional picture is correct.

But was it Matthew who constructed the passage, or is the whole of the chapter taken from a source with only minor redactional modification? Since the goal of this study has been defined as discovering what the author has done, it would normally be necessary to wait until further analyses are complete in order to have grounds for comparison and thus a basis from which to answer the question. But there is another means of verification in this case. The linear analysis has shown that the writer of this portion of Matthew held a very special view of the parables and their meaning. According to this view the parables are veiled statements about the coming kingdom of heaven and its consequences. If this is the view of the author of the whole gospel, it should be reflected in his use of other parables.

It has already been observed (above, p. 27) that Matthew applies the introductory formula of kingdom comparison to four of his other parables. However, the relationship between the parables discourse and Matthew's use of the parables is far more extensive than just in the introduction of four other parables. There are 18 extensive parables in Matthew. They appear from 7:24 in the Sermon on the Mount, throughout the gospel until the Judgment scene in 25:31ff. Of these 18, all are parables of the kingdom or of judgment or are so interpreted by Matthew, except the one in the discourse on discipleship, the parable of the Lost Sheep (18:10–14). Matthew consistently regards the parables as veiled comments about the coming judgment. Even the Lost Sheep takes on an eschatological dimension by Matthew's comment, "It is not the will of your Father in heaven that one of these little ones should perish" (18:14). "Perish" (**ἀπόληται**) probably refers to eschatological death and punishment.[42]

The consequence of Matthew's stress upon the eschatological dimension of the parables is readily evident. It goes a long way toward explaining why he has a more limited spectrum of the parables than does Luke. Matthew would have been hard pressed to make some of the Lucan parables fit his parable theory, for example, the parable of the Good Samaritan. Matthew believed that Jesus' parables were told in order to reveal to the disciples the secrets of the end-time and all of his use of the parables reflects the theory established in 13:10–17. This provides strong evidence that the writer who shaped the parables discourse is the author of the gospel.

THE ANALYSIS AND THE SYNOPTIC PROBLEM

The linear analysis of Mt 13:1–52 has shown the well organized character of this literary unit. Much of the material in the section is paralleled in Mark and Luke.[43] A complete appraisal of the results of this analysis for source criticism is not feasible here, but a number of problems may be listed as important for further discussion.

Some of the evidence from the analysis supports the view that Matthew may have used Mark as the basis for his discourse. The choice of the parable of the Sower and the order of the first three sections (Sower, theory, and interpretation of the Sower) point in that direction. The presence of the conclusion to Mark's discourse in the midst of the Matthean passage may also be cited as evidence for the use of Mark as a foundation for the discourse.

On the other hand, a number of the results of the analysis also point to the need for a measure of rethinking with regard to the traditional solution that

42. W. Bauer, W. F. Arndt, and F. W. Gingrich, *A Greek-English Lexicon of the New Testament* (Chicago: University of Chicago Press, 1957), 94.

43. Most of the parallels are found in Mk 4 and Lk 8, but portions are also paralleled in Lk 10 and 13.

Matthew has built the discourse from Mark, Q, and some of his own special tradition. At precisely the point where Matthew formulates his unique theory of interpretation of the parables there is a rather extensive agreement of Matthew and Luke against Mark (Mt 13:11 // Lk 8:10: ὑμῖν δέδοται γνῶναι τὰ μυστήρια, Mk 4:11: ὑμῖν τὸ μυστήριον δέδοται). Also, the key word connection of the Blessing saying, Mt 13:16–17 // Lk 10:23–24, to the Isa 6:9–10 text (at least 10 words in the two verses) may suggest that it originated in the Matthean (or a similar) context. If this is true, some adjustment would be required in the Q hypothesis.[44] And finally, the literary evidence for the existence of a source behind Matthew's kingdom parables raises some important questions about the source of Mustard Seed and Conclusion in Mk 4:30–33 and Mustard Seed and Leaven in Lk 13:18–21.[45]

More fascinating for future research than these results is the question of the overlapping of redactional motif as an indication of literary dependence.[46] For example, do elements of Matthew's special theory of interpretation of the parables appear in Mark and Luke even though they are not employed meaningfully by those authors? Or, does the Marcan theory of the Messianic secret appear in Matthew and Luke and thereby betray their use of Mark?

The linear analysis of Mt 13 has apparently opened some fascinating new avenues for exploration by source critics.

THE ANALYSIS AND AN UNDERSTANDING OF MATTHEW

The linear analysis has brought to light a number of important features of Matthew's thought. It has shown that he is able to use the OT to shape the gospel material. Moreover, it has revealed a measure of subtlety on the part of Matthew as he uses the OT, takes items out of context, and interprets them to suit his own particular interests and needs. Isa 6:9–10, which speaks only of the blindness of the people, is used to make a contrast between the blindness of the people and the insight of the disciples. Ps 78:2 is taken entirely out of context and interpreted as a reference to the parables of Jesus

44. The problem is acute if Mt's relation to Q is viewed in B. H. Streeter's manner, "If we consider . . . the fact . . . that sayings like 'Blessed are your eyes,' Mt xiii, 16–17 . . . being imbedded in extracts from Mark—cannot possibly be in their original context as they occur in Matthew, the presumption is plainly in favor of the view that Luke's order is the more original" *The Four Gospels* (London: Macmillan and Co., 1924), 275.

45. A number of solutions are possible. The suggested source could be proven not to exist; the kingdom parables and conclusion may have been a part of Q and this another instance of Mk/Q overlap; multiple sources for these short parables may have existed; or Mk and Lk may have used Mt.

46. To my knowledge this question has not been discussed by source critics at the level of direct literary evidence, but on the level of hypothetical motivation for alterations. It would seem that the phenomenon of redactional overlap would only be useful to the source critic if it could be demonstrated directly in the text.

and their revelations of the secrets of the end-time. This is not an irreverent attitude toward the OT. The scribes of Qumran were equally free with the OT both in shaping the text and in interpreting it. So were the apocalyticists of whatever sort.[47] So, indeed, were the Rabbis.[48] All of them combined a deep reverence for the OT as revelation with a remarkably free and even manipulative method of interpretation. Matthew's use of the OT, as revealed by the analysis, reflects the uses in first-century Judaism.

Much more distinctive of Matthew is his attitude toward the authority of the parables of Jesus. This analysis has shown an attitude on the part of Matthew toward the parables which is quite distinct from viewing them as legal prescriptions. The role of the parables was for Matthew the same as the role the prophetic writings held in Qumran. Hidden within the parables, Matthew believed, were the secrets of the end-time and those secrets were discernible for the one who was a disciple, a scribe trained for the kingdom of heaven. Matthew treats the parables as sacred texts in the sense that they reveal a message from God and about God's will. He consistently treats the parables, even (as in the Sower) when they resist his efforts, as veiled statements of the coming end of the age.

The eschatological interpretation of the parables touches a fundamental element in Matthew's thought. The emphasis on the future judgment in Matthew has long been recognized.[49] Matthew is a thinker who is strongly influenced by an ethical dualism which pits the evil against the good in a struggle that will be concluded only at the judgment. This means that one way of working toward an understanding of his work in the gospel is to trace the consistency of the ethical and eschatological dualism.

In his use of the OT, in his interpretation of the parables along apocalyptic lines, and in his emphasis on eschatology, Matthew reveals himself to have been a Jewish-Christian who was quite at home in the thought world of first-century Judaism. The predominance of eschatological interest in this portion of the gospel should not lead to the conclusion that Matthew's major Jewish influences were apocalyptic or sectarian. Much more evidence from other portions of the gospel must be considered before a statement of the specific influences on Matthew can be made. At this point the linear analysis of the parable discourse has only revealed a Jewish-Christian scholar at work. He is a man with a knowledge of the OT text and of the Jewish ways of interpreting it. He is a creative thinker who provides a logical structure for the discourse that is peculiarly his own.

47. See B. J. Roberts, "The Dead Sea Scrolls and the O.T. Scriptures," *BJRL* 36 (1953) 75–96, on the similarities of interpretation between the scrolls and the apocalyptic writings.

48. The careful system of hermeneutics developed by the Rabbis was designed to allow greater breadth of interpretation (See Hermann Strack, *Introduction to Talmud and Midrash* [2nd ed., New York: Harper and Row, 1965], 93–98).

49. The work of Bornkamm and Barth in *Tradition and Interpretation in Matthew*, 15–164, concentrates on this aspect of Mt's interest.

ANALYSIS 2: MT 12 AND THE ROLE OF ISA 42:1–4

Ch. 12 is an appropriate place for a second test of the hypothesis that Matthew shapes his gospel by using the OT texts. Here a citation occurs in the midst of a chapter which has never yielded an orderly structure to other types of investigation. The citation is peculiar to Matthew and is introduced by his citation formula, "This was to fulfill what was spoken by the prophet Isaiah." If it can be shown that this text has some logical connection to the structure of the chapter, and if a linear analysis can be accomplished which illumines the work of the author in the chapter, a further step in Matthean redaction criticism may be made.

The outline of the chapter:

1–8	The debate over eating corn on the Sabbath
9–13	The debate over healing on the Sabbath
14	The Pharisees plot to destroy Jesus
15–16	Jesus withdraws and counsels his followers to silence
17–21	The formula citation of Isa 42:1–4
22–23	Jesus heals a blind and dumb demoniac
24–37	A controversy with the Pharisees over the healing
38–41	The scribes ask a sign and are reminded of Jonah
42	The queen of the South
43–45	The fate of the man whose unclean spirit returned
46–50	The mother and brothers of Jesus seek him

A preliminary form-critical analysis reveals a striking variety of material in these 50 verses. The first two pericopes are identifiable as apophthegms (Bultmann's term)[50] or pronouncement stories (V. Taylor's terminology).[51] They both deal with the question of Jesus' orthodoxy or unorthodoxy as regards the Sabbath regulations. The next two elements are not original to the stories. The plotting response of the Pharisees and Jesus' decision to seek refuge are a narrative connection which has been added to the stories. At what stage in the tradition this occurred cannot as yet be determined.

At this point Matthew introduces the formula citation of Isa 42:1. The form of the citation and its reason for being in this place must be carefully considered in the linear analysis.

The next major section of the chapter is introduced by a simple miracle story (vss. 22–23). It is so simple, in fact, that it could be considered an

50. Bultmann, *History of the Synoptic Tradition,* 12 and 16–17.

51. V. Taylor, *The Gospel According to St. Mark* (London: Macmillan and Co., Ltd., 1963), 212 and 220.

exemplar for the miracle story stripped to the bare essentials: the demoniac and his ailments, the healing by Jesus, the response of the people. This story serves to introduce a sharp debate between Jesus and the Pharisees over the source of Jesus' healings and exorcisms. The material in the debate is not uniform. Jesus' replies in vss. 25–37 are partially parabolic, e.g., the kingdom divided (vss. 25–26) and the tree and its fruit (vs. 33), and give evidence of being formed from existing traditions. How much is tradition and how much redaction and how they are woven together must also be a concern of the linear analysis.

The next section is a debate introduced by the request for a sign from Jesus. The reply cites the example of Jonah as justification for the refusal to give a sign. The following passage dealing with the queen of the South has exactly the same comparative form as the Jonah reply and may have been a part of a tradition in which it accompanied the Jonah comparison. These verses are followed by a strange piece of material relating the fate of one whose unclean spirit returns with friends to the fate of the present generation (vss. 43–45). The place of this odd passage in the chapter must also concern the redaction analysis.

The final pericope of the chapter is the story of the attempt of the family of Jesus to see him and his refusal to go to them. In its present form it is a pronouncement story. The linear analysis must also deal with the question of how this pericope fits into the chapter and concludes it.

The best way to begin following Matthew's construction of this chapter is to look at the relationship of the citation text to the material which precedes it. What has led Matthew to cite Isa 42:1–4 as a fulfillment of prophecy? In the analysis of ch. 13, the citation of Ps 78:2 was prompted by the sentence immediately preceding it. This phenomenon suggests that perhaps the connections for the citations are directly made to the immediate context. A brief examination of the citations in chs. 1 and 2 of the gospel confirms this suggestion. The five citations there are without exception related to the preceding sentence. Thus one possibility for a relation of text to context is a close connection between Isa 42:1–4 and the immediately preceding verse:

> Jesus, aware of this [the plot of the Pharisees, vs. 14], withdrew from there. And many followed him, and he healed them all, and ordered them not to make him known. This was to fulfill what was spoken by the prophet Isaiah:
> "Behold, my servant whom I have chosen,
> my beloved with whom my soul is well pleased.
> I will put my Spirit upon him,
> and he shall proclaim justice to the Gentiles.
> He will not wrangle or cry aloud,
> nor will anyone hear his voice in the streets;
> he will not break a bruised reed
> or quench a smoldering wick,
> till he brings justice to victory;
> and in his name will the Gentiles hope" 12:15ff.).

There is nothing in the first two couplets of the Isaiah text which can be related to the preceding sentences. Nothing has been said about the servant or about the Messiah. Nothing has been said about the Spirit or about the Gentiles. If Matthew is relating the text to 12:15–16, no clue to that relationship is found in these verses of the Isaiah text.

It is in the next verse of the citation Mt 12:19/Isa 42:2 that the connection emerges:

> He will not wrangle or cry aloud,
> nor will anyone hear his voice in the streets;
> he will not break a bruised reed
> or quench a smoldering wick,
> till he brings justice to victory;
> and in his name will the Gentiles hope.

Jesus has purposely withdrawn from public view because of the plot of the Pharisees. That plot was hardly an assassination plot, but rather one aimed at trapping Jesus in some political offense and thus destroying him.[52] Jesus chooses not to play their game. At least that is the way this tradition draws the picture and, apparently, as Matthew understands it. He retires into relative seclusion, and, although found out by the sick whom he heals and commands to silence, his intention is withdrawal. Matthew sees this action as fulfillment of the prophet's words, "He will not wrangle or cry aloud, nor will anyone hear his voice in the streets." Stendahl strongly urges this connection on the basis of the changes Matthew has made in the text of this verse (**ἐρίσει** is peculiar to Mt in the text traditions and "nor will anyone hear his voice" has been made active in voice).[53] If this is true, the major connection of the text to context would be the concept of the retiring character of the servant. He refuses to put himself forward.

An alternative suggestion for the relationship may also be considered. It is possible that the immediate context does not provide the connective. Is there something in 12:1–13 which suggests the prophecy to Matthew? It has been argued that the rationale for the text lies in the healings of 9–13 and 15 which testify to Jesus' messiahship.[54] If that were true, however, the reader should expect Matthew to provide some readily identifiable clue to the connection. There is none. The stories in 12:1–13 provide evidence for the growing

52. This is true in both Mt and Mk. The plot pre-figures the passion events. It is perhaps even clearer in Mk where the Herodians are included in the scheme and heighten the sense of political intrigue, Mk 3:6.

53. Stendahl, *School*, 110–115. It is true that Mt's hand on the text itself is most readily apparent in this verse, but Mt has very carefully shaped the first couplet also, so that one cannot argue on this basis alone.

54. This is the position taken by E. Lohmeyer in *Das Evangelium des Matthäus*, ed. by W. Schmauch (Göttingen: Vandenhoeck and Ruprecht, 1962), 186–187. However, he offers no connection between the citation and the preceding verses.

hostility of the Pharisees and the reason for their plot. They do not provide a basis for the citation of Isa 42:1–4.

The most direct connection which can be observed between the Isaiah citation and its context is, therefore, Jesus' refusal to put himself forward. This is fulfilled in the prophecy that "he will not wrangle or cry aloud."[55] Both the logic and the fact that this direct connection is similar to the one observed for the Ps 78:2 citation support this view.[56]

It is difficult to work backward from this connection in order to trace the hand of Matthew in the first 13 verses of the chapter. Both of the stories are very briefly introduced. One portion of the first story may safely be assigned to Matthew, however. In 9:13 Matthew made a point of having Jesus say, "Go and learn what this means, 'I desire mercy, and not sacrifice.'" When this line is repeated, quite out of context even if appropriately in Matthew's eyes (see below, Analysis 5), in 12:7, it is probably an insertion by Matthew into the original story. Moreover, the line, "I tell you, something greater than the temple is here," which has formal parallels in 12:41 and 42, also appears to be a Matthean insertion which interrupts the story.

It has also been suggested that vss. 11–12a are an insertion by Matthew.[57] However, a word of caution is in order because the commentators fail to notice the *a fortiori* argument which is involved.[58] "Of how much more value is a man than a sheep!" (12a). This provides a rationale for healing on the Sabbath which the bald statement, "So it is lawful to do good on the sabbath," does not provide. It is difficult to say whether the whole argument of vss. 11–12 or only the last line (as in Mark) belonged to the tradition. But for the most part, Matthew has been following traditional material in the opening portion of the chapter. It is now appropriate to ask whether the citation has any effect on the material which follows.

The material which caused Matthew to cite Isa 42:1–4 and Matthew's own reason for the citation spoke of a withdrawal on the part of Jesus, a refusal to put himself forward in the face of Pharisaic opposition. In that light, it is remarkable that the very next pericope presents Jesus in a new conflict with

55. Stendahl is not alone in this view. See also A. H. McNeile, *The Gospel According to St. Matthew* (New York: St. Martin's Press, 1965), 172–173; and A. Schlatter, *Das Evangelium nach Matthäus: Erlauterungen zum Neuen Testament* (Band 1, Stuttgart: Calwer Verlag, 1961), 192–193.

56. Another way of approaching the problem would be to observe that all of Mt's other citations are so obvious as to be trite. Mt must have thought this one to be fairly obvious also. The connection suggested, while hardly trite, at least does not strain the evidence or the context as the alternative must do.

57. Bultmann, *History of the Synoptic Tradition,* 12, and McNeile, *Matthew,* 170.

58. The relevance of the problem of mercy to animals in Jewish tradition about Sabbath regulations is amply illustrated in H. L. Strack and P. Billerbeck, *Kommentar zum Neuen Testament aus Talmud und Midrasch* (München: C. H. Beck, 1926), I, 629–630. On the "if this . . . how much the more so" argument see Strack, *Introduction to Talmud and Midrash,* 94, on *Kal vachomer.*

the Pharisees. The line of logic which brought this material together cannot be that of a straightforward narrative. Something has caused an abrupt change of narrative direction.

The Isaiah citation provides a clue to the organization of the passage. The material which follows the citation consists of a miracle story followed by a sharp exchange between Jesus and the Pharisees. The Pharisees charge that "it is only by Beelzebul, the prince of demons, that this man casts out demons" (12:24). Jesus replies initially with the analogy of the kingdom, or city, or household that is divided, and then with the argument, "if I cast out demons by Beelzebul, by whom do your sons cast them out? Therefore they shall be your judges. But if it is by the Spirit of God that I cast out demons, then the kingdom of God has come upon you" (12:27–28). From this verse through vs. 32, the subject is the Holy Spirit.

Why this debate, in these terms, occurs here is the question the redaction critic must ask. An answer may be found in the opening lines of the Isaiah citation. Therefore, an analysis of those lines is in order:

> Behold, my servant whom I have chosen,
> my beloved with whom my soul is well pleased.
> I will put my Spirit upon him,
> and he shall proclaim justice to the Gentiles (vs. 18).

That Matthew understands the text as a reference to the Messiah seems to be clear. The Targum translation of the opening verse (עבדי משיחא) "my servant, the Messiah . . ." attests to the use of the passage as a Messianic text in Judaism.[59] The rest of the opening line reflects the Isaiah text. But the second line corresponds not so much to any OT text as it does to the words of the voice from heaven at Jesus' baptism.

"This is my beloved son with whom I am well pleased" (3:17). Matthew's ἀγαπητός, "beloved," has no counterpart in any known text and the "well pleased" only in a variant LXX text. It is strongly to be suspected that Matthew has reshaped the opening lines to agree closely with the voice at the baptism in order to have the reader recall the messiahship of Jesus.[60]

This text makes two promises about the servant who has been chosen by God. 1) He will have the Spirit of God, and 2) he will proclaim justice to the Gentiles. If anyone makes a claim to fulfilling this prophecy, he must show that these promises are fulfilled. This is the background of Matthew's construction of the rest of the chapter.

In view of this Matthean application of a Messianic text to Jesus, the response of the people to the healing of the blind and dumb demoniac

59. Targum Jonathan to Isa 42:1. See J. Jeremias, "Παῖς Θεοῦ," *TDNT,* V, ed. by G. Friedrich, Eng. trans. by G. Bromiley (1967), 681. He also notes the same translation of servant in 43:10 and 52:13. For the common connection of the Davidic Messiah and servanthood, cf. Ezek 37:24, "David, my servant. . . ."

60. Stendahl, *School,* 109–111, argues decisively for the connection.

(12:23) takes on new importance. They ask, "Can this be the Son of David?" The puzzled but awed response of the people to the exorcism is phrased as a question of Messiahship. Against the possibility that Jesus is the Messiah the Pharisees retort, "It is only by Beelzebul, the prince of demons, that this man casts out demons." Their charge against Jesus is not that he is himself demon-possessed (it is understood thus only by Mark in 3:22 and 30), but that Jesus is able to control the lesser demons because of his contact with the prince of demons. The charge reflects the popular belief that magicians were only able to perform their wonders by special contact with the occult world, the world of demons.[61] It also reflects the firmly attested Jewish charge that Jesus was a magician, or sorcerer.[62] Matthew has already mentioned this controversy in 9:34 and 10:25. Now, in the context of a prophecy of the gift of the Holy Spirit to the Messiah, he takes up the debate in earnest.

Jesus' reply to the charge of collusion with Beelzebul is a series of sayings. Because of their complex relationships, they deserve special attention. The answer may be outlined as follows:

25–26 The charge of collusion is compared to the state of a divided kingdom, or city, or household.
27–28 Jesus asks the source of Pharisaic healings, and poses the alternative that his healings are signs of the kingdom.
29 The analogy of how to rob a strong man.
30 The "with me or against me" saying.
31–32 On blasphemy against the Holy Spirit.
33–35 How evil cannot produce good.
36–37 Judgment will be based on what one has spoken.

Even this outline, which I have partially shaped to fit what I believe to be the flow of Matthew's logic, does not readily reveal the argument which has been marshalled against the opponents. It must be traced more carefully.

The initial thrust of the reply is to make the charge of collusion with Beelzebul logically absurd. Jesus cites a series of analogies:

> 25 Every kingdom divided against itself is laid waste, and no city or house divided against itself will stand;
>
> 26 and if Satan casts out Satan, he is divided against himself; how then will his kingdom stand?

This answer is carefully and logically employed. However, as W. Foerster has noted, it makes some changes in the premises. Popular belief in demons was not so monolithic that all demons were believed to be controlled by

61. W. Foerster, "Δαίμων," *TDNT,* II, 1–21, describes the belief that the magician achieves real contact with the demon. See also *The Jewish Encyclopedia,* ed. by I. Singer (New York: Fund and Wagnalls, 1901), III, 517ff., on demonology.

62. Strack-Billerbeck, I, 631.

Satan.[63] Beelzebul may have been the prince, and the most powerful demon, but this answer presupposes a far more dualistic theory of demons than the challenge is likely to have presupposed. Nevertheless, the logic is clear and unimpeachable if the presuppositions are granted.

With the absurdity of the charge established, the second rebuttal serves to heighten the effect. "If I cast out demons by Beelzebul, by whom do your sons [Pharisaic exorcists] cast them out?" Since the Pharisaic rules on such matters were not consistent and some Rabbis were famous as exorcists,[64] the point is well taken.

The next line is the crux of the rebuttal of the Pharisees' charge. The absurdity of the charge that Jesus casts out demons by the power of Beelzebul has been established. The consequence to be drawn is this, "But if it is by the Spirit of God that I cast out demons, then the kingdom of God has come upon you." There is a great logical hurdle here. Why should Jesus' exorcisms mean anything other than Pharisaic exorcisms? The answer lies in an assumption which does not appear in the argument. It is the contention that Jesus is the Messiah and activity on his part done by the power of the Holy Spirit would prove it, because this is promised to the Messiah in Isa 42:2, "I will pour out my Spirit upon him." In other words, if the Pharisees' charge is wrong, then the people's response is right and Jesus is the Son of David, *and* the kingdom is dawning in the deeds of Jesus. This is very tight logic involving the people's response, the Pharisees' charge, the rebuttal, and the consequence as an instance of the promise of Isa 42.

The next verses return to the all-or-nothing theme. The first step is an argument concerning what one must do to rob a strong man. In like manner Jesus has conquered Satan and is now robbing his house of those held captive by the demons. There is no such thing as collusion with the enemy. "He who is not with me is against me, and he who does not gather with me scatters." With that reply the charge against Jesus begins to turn back against the opponents themselves.

Jesus now (vss. 31–32) turns to the offensive:

> Therefore I tell you, every sin and blasphemy will be forgiven men, but blasphemy against the Spirit will not be forgiven. And whoever says a word against the Son of Man will be forgiven, but whoever speaks against the Holy Spirit will not be forgiven, either in this age or the age to come.

The progress of the linear analysis up to this point provides the key to an understanding of this highly controversial saying.[65] The Pharisees had not

63. Foerster, "Δαίμων," 18.

64. Even R. Jochanan b. Zakkai was reputed to be able to understand the language of the demons *(B. Talmud, Sukka 28a)*.

65. The saying has, of course, been theologically offensive as well as exegetically difficult. For an attempt to analyze away the offense, see O. Evans, "The Unforgivable Sin," *ExpT* 68 (1957) 240–244.

made a direct accusation against the miracles of Jesus but had instead maligned the force by which he performed them. Here Jesus accepts those terms of debate. By providing a general rule which all could accept and then giving an instance related to this debate, the Pharisees' charge is shown to be blasphemous.

> The general rule:
>
> Therefore I tell you, every sin and blasphemy will be forgiven men, but blasphemy against the Spirit will not be forgiven.

In this context Spirit clearly means Holy Spirit, and as such it was a way of speaking of God. All would agree that blasphemy against God was unforgivable.[66]

> The application:
>
> Whoever says a word against the Son of Man will be forgiven; but whoever speaks against the Holy Spirit will not be forgiven, either in this age or in the age to come.[67]

At first glance this is little more than a restatement of the preceding sentence. But when it is taken seriously in the context of the debate, a subtle but forceful logic emerges. It would have been excusable for the Pharisees to have spoken against Jesus himself. But they have not. Instead, they impugned the power by which he works. By this logical reply, Matthew has had Jesus show that the deeds cannot have been done by the power of Beelzebul but were done by the power of the Holy Spirit. That means that the Pharisees have called the Holy Spirit the prince of demons and have committed an unforgivable blasphemy.[68]

The guilt of the Pharisees is thus established. So the reply proceeds to an attack upon them and their words. First the Pharisees are compared to a tree in the metaphor "good tree–good fruit, bad tree–bad fruit" (cf. the same image in 7:17ff. applied to false prophets). The fruit of the Pharisees is their blasphemy against the Holy Spirit. What further evidence is needed of their nature? The fruits analogy is applied directly to men in vss. 34–35. A final statement warns ominously of the dire consequences of such rash charges as the one the Pharisees have made. "For by your words you will be justified and by your words you will be condemned" (vs. 37).

From the miracle story which introduced the debate to the closing sentence, the linear reading of the Beelzebul controversy in Matthew has shown a consistent, highly organized argument which has been constructed

66. This was not the *only* unforgivable sin in Judaism, see *Pirke Aboth* 3:11 for others. Strack-Billerbeck, I, 637.

67. The best available treatment of these verses and the connection of blasphemy to the Holy Spirit and the Beelzebul charge is that by McNeile (*Matthew*, 178–179).

68. That this is the meaning of the two verses is seen by Taylor (*Mark*, 242) even though the context is less clear in Mk because there are two charges in Mk.

as support for the claim that the line in the Isaiah citation, "I will pour out my Spirit upon him," applies to Jesus.

The next pericope begins with a request by scribes and Pharisees for a sign (vs. 38). Once again there is a lack of direct narrative thread. Indeed, in the reply to this request Jesus refuses (vs. 39) to give any sign but one:

> An evil and adulterous generation seeks a sign; but no sign shall be given to it except the sign of the prophet Jonah.

In the Beelzebul controversy it was clear that the exorcisms were to be understood as signs of Jesus' messiahship. "But if it is by the Spirit of God that I cast out demons, then the kingdom of God has come upon you." The juxtaposition of these passages suggests that the Jonah pericope is not directly connected to the Beelzebul account. It certainly does not follow smoothly in the same line of thought.

An immediate clue to an understanding of the pericope lies in the nature of the question and the identity of the questioners. Since it was the Pharisees who were so strongly attacked in the prior account, it is not surprising to find them here. Matthew has every reason to bring them along. But the scribes are new and they are the key to the question. Their request for a sign is a request for exegetical confirmation, for a sign which can be verified by the scribes whose job is to interpret the Scriptures (cf. the same exegetical inquiry in John 6:30ff.). The reply made by Jesus is a stern refusal to be bound by the scribal rules for Messianic identification.

A problem similar to that of the original text in Mt 13:14–15 now arises. The statement of refusal save for the sign of Jonah is followed in the text by the following sentences:

> For as Jonah was three days and three nights in the belly of the whale, so will the Son of man be three days and three nights in the heart of the earth. The men of Nineveh will arise at the judgment with this generation and condemn it; for they repented at the preaching of Jonah, and behold, something greater than Jonah is here (vss. 40f.).

This has always been a difficult passage to understand. There are two things about Jonah mentioned; the sojourn in the whale and his preaching to Nineveh. If the first is the sign intended, then it seems to conform to the questioners' wish for a dramatic sign capable of being tested exegetically (whether it would have been understood as Messianic is not clear.).[69] But then the final part of the saying would be superfluous. If however, the final note about the Ninevites is intended, then the sign is not at all in accord with

69. The evidence that the early church struggled to find an OT prophecy of the resurrection on the third day is very clear, cf. 1 Cor 15:3ff. See B. Lindars, *New Testament Apologetic* (London: SCM Press, 1961), 59ff.

the request and the rebuke to the questioners is justified. This solution would make the "three days and nights" reference extraneous.

There are reasons to question the authenticity to Matthew of the "three days and three nights" reference. Stendahl gives them as follows: 1) With 13:14–15, this is the only other instance of a literal citation of the LXX. 2) The Jonah quotation breaks the continuity between vs. 39 and vs. 41. The "wicked and adulterous generation" of vs. 39 parallels "the Ninevites" of vs. 41 and Jonah of vs. 39 clearly leads to "one greater than Jonah" in vs. 41. In *Dialogue with Trypho* 107:1f., Justin Martyr quotes this passage from Matthew but without the Jonah quotation.[70]

There are two arguments for caution in assigning this text to a post-Matthean copyist, however. First, the text tradition is unanimous in its support of the reading of vs. 40 in its present form and context in Matthew. Second, as McNeile has argued, Justin may have wished to avoid the embarrassment of the chronological difficulty in "three days and three nights" and therefore have omitted the verse.[71]

On further analysis, however, these arguments for caution lose a great deal of force. Since none of the extant texts for this portion of Matthew can be dated earlier than the fourth century,[72] this evidence may mean that the insertion had occurred later than the work of Justin, c. 150 A.D. Much more important is the fact that the full context of Justin's use of the passage from Matthew renders McNeile's position extremely doubtful.

Justin says:

> And that he would rise again on the third day after the crucifixion, it is written in the memoirs that some of your nation, questioning him, said, "Show us a sign," and he replied to them, "An evil and adulterous generation seeketh after a sign; and no sign shall be given them, save the sign of Jonah." And since he spoke this obscurely (*καὶ ταῦτα λέγοντος αὐτοῦ παρακεκαλυμμένα*),[73] it was to be understood by the audience that after his crucifixion he should rise again on the third day. And he showed that your generation was more wicked and more adulterous than the city of Nineveh. . . .[74]

Two things are clear here. According to Justin, Jesus replied with vs. 39 of Matthew's text and went on "to show" the parallel of Nineveh to that

70. It should be noted that Stendahl implies that vs. 41 is quoted by Justin. It is not. See Stendahl (*School* 132–133) for these arguments.

71. McNeile, *Matthew*, 181–182.

72. For the dating of the manuscripts see B. Metzger, *The Text of the New Testament* (Oxford: Clarendon Press, 1964), 36ff. The earliest extant manuscripts of this portion of Mt are the 4th-cent. uncials. Two centuries of text tradition between Justin and our manuscripts weaken the argument from the unanimity of the texts.

73. Greek text is from *Patrologiae Cursus Completus—Series Graeca*, Vol. 6, ed. by J. P. Migne (Paris: 1857), 724–725.

74. English trans., *The Ante-Nicene Fathers*, I, ed. by Roberts and Donaldson (American ed. revised by A. C. Coxe, Grand Rapids: Wm B. Eerdmans, 1950), 252–253.

generation,[75] but it was necessary for the audience "to understand" (ἦν νοεῖσθαι) the sign of Jonah as reference to the resurrection. It is very hard to believe that he would not have used Mt 12:40, which suits his purpose so well, if it had stood in his text of Matthew. There is no indication here that Justin is reluctant to use the three days and three nights chronology, although he does use the more traditional "on the third day." Justin only says that the mysterious statement of Jesus should be understood as a reference to the resurrection.

Stronger confirmation for the view that 12:40 did not stand in the original text of Matthew is provided by a linear reading of the passage in the context. The Beelzebul controversy has established the messiahship of Jesus as the one on whom the Spirit rests. The second promise to the Messiah in the Isa 42 text is, "And he will announce justice to the Gentiles." When Mt 12:38,39, and 41 are read as a unit, a relationship becomes clear. The men of Nineveh, a fine example of Gentiles, had been preached to by Jonah, and "lo, one greater than Jonah is here."[76] Moreover, Jonah had announced justice to the Ninevites, "Yet forty days and Nineveh shall be overthrown" (Jon 3:4).

The passage draws a parallel between the work of Jonah and that of Jesus. However, it is not readily apparent how that relationship exists. In Matthew's account of the activities of the earthly Jesus there is no mission to the Gentiles. Only reluctantly does Jesus agree to heal the Canaanite woman's daughter (15:21ff.). The only other healing in which a Gentile figures is that of the centurion's daughter in 8:5–13. The mission of the disciples (ch. 10) is limited to "the lost sheep of the house of Israel." There is no tradition in Matthew of a proclamation of justice to the Gentiles by the earthly Jesus.

However, so neat a distinction between the activities of the earthly Jesus and the risen Lord is probably invalid. The promise to the servant in Isa 42:1–4 is a future one (ἀπαγγελεῖ), and there is no reason to confine that future to the present of Jesus or of Matthew. There is a scene in Matthew where Jesus announces justice to the Gentiles (or nations), 25:31–46. There Jesus as the Son of Man has taken his place as the Messianic king upon his throne and announces the final judgment of the nations. It has been said that the sign of Jonah in 12:38–41 means the preaching of repentance.[77] But Jonah preached only judgment.[78] In fact, Jonah is very angry when Nineveh repents and God withholds punishment. Or it has been claimed that Jesus,

75. A. J. Bellinzoni, in *The Sayings of Jesus in the Writings of Justin Martyr* (Leiden: E. J. Brill, 1967), 121, demonstrates conclusively that 107:1 and Mt 16:4 lack the words **τοῦ προφήτου** at the end of the sentence; Bellinzoni thinks this is the source of the Justin quotation. But the rest of the paragraph in Justin clearly presupposes Mt 12:41, and requires that the passage cited be Mt 12:38–42.

76. For the neuter **πλεῖον** understood as masculine, N. Turner, *Grammar of New Testament Greek*, III (Edinburgh: T. & T. Clark, 1963), 21.

77. Schlatter, *Das Evangelium nach Matthäus*, 203.

78. Jonah's words were, "Yet forty days and I will destroy Nineveh" (3:4).

like Jonah, comes from a far country (heaven?) to proclaim God's word.[79] Such an argument defies the simple geography of the setting. The function of Jonah was the announcing of justice to the Ninevites. In Matthew's view, Jesus is greater than Jonah and will one day announce justice to the Gentiles, thus fulfilling the second promise to the Messiah made in Isa 42:1–4. This is certainly Matthew's work because it combines Matthean motifs (the Jonah sign and the judgment of the nations) in a logical way in order to connect the passage to the external source, Isa 42:1–4.[80]

With Matthew's redactional purpose in view, it is possible to make a tradition-redaction separation in vss. 38–42. The doublet of the sign request in 16:1–4 is of great help. It is parallel to this passage except for two features. 1) The Sadducees have replaced the scribes. 2) There is no explanation of the enigmatic refusal of any sign but that of Jonah. This was probably the basic form of a Christian tradition which claimed the resurrection as a sign which should end such scribal speculation. Matthew has made the pericope fit his purpose in ch. 12 by adding to it the tradition about the reaction of the Ninevites to Jonah in vs. 41 and connecting it to the promise made to the Messiah in Isa 42:2. Thus, Matthew's understanding of vs. 41 is the key to the redactional structure of the passage.

There is further evidence that vss. 41–42 are traditional. Although vs. 41 serves Matthew's interest here, the saying about Solomon is irrelevant to this context. It has precisely the same form as the Jonah saying and was probably, therefore, attached to it in the tradition employed by Matthew. Taken together these sayings make a point entirely different from either that of the sign pericope of 16:1–4 or the use Matthew has made of the Jonah saying in this context. They point to the reaction of non-Jews to a former Jewish prophet and a former Jewish king and declare that Jesus is greater than either Jonah or Solomon. In 12:6 the very same final line appears, "I say to you something greater than the temple is here." The suggestion is natural that Matthew has used a tradition which cited the response of three different non-Jewish groups or persons to the temple, to the prophet Jonah, and to king Solomon. Perhaps it went like this:

> Hiram of Sidon will arise at the judgment and condemn this generation; for Hiram carried timbers to Jerusalem for constructing the temple and behold, something greater than the temple is here.
>
> The men of Nineveh will arise at the judgment with this generation and condemn it; for they repented at the preaching of Jonah, and behold, something greater than Jonah is here.

79. J. M. Creed, *The Gospel According to St. Luke* (New York: St. Martin's Press, 1965), 162–163; and Bultmann, *History of the Synoptic Tradition*, 118.

80. I retain the term "justice" to point out the connection with the Isaianic promise. That Mt understands justice in the forensic sense of passing judgment is, however, evident in the context.

> The queen of the South will arise at the judgment with this generation and condemn it; for she came from the ends of the earth to hear the wisdom of Solomon, and behold, something greater than Solomon is here.

Although this reconstruction is highly speculative, such a tradition might have had its origins in the attempt of the church to understand how the contemporaries of Jesus, and even their own Jewish contemporaries, could fail to see in Jesus the fulfillment of the Messianic hopes, to see in him one who was greater than any of the old traditions.[81] Matthew has employed two parts of the tradition to suit his own purposes but reveals the existence of some such tradition by employing the "queen of the South" logion without appropriate context.

The next pericope in Matthew is one of the most difficult to interpret in all of the gospels, 12:43–45. It is a mysterious little story of the fate of an unfortunate man who had a demon cast out only to have the demon go and get his friends and return to the man. This left the poor fellow in worse shape than before.

How did this little bit of tradition happen to be attached to this context in Matthew? The clue lies in the concluding verse (45):

> And the last state of the man was worse than the first.
> Thus it will be for this evil generation.

The last sentence is unquestionably a Matthean addition, for nothing has been said about this evil generation in the story itself. The generation was important, however, in the preceding material:

> An evil and adulterous generation seeks for a sign (vs. 39).
>
> . . . will arise at the judgment with this generation and condemn it (vss. 41, 42).

The connection between the story of the returning demon and the theme of a wicked generation is this: The present state of this generation is bad enough in its ignorance and hostility to Jesus the Messiah, but its fate at the judgment will be much worse. "And the last state of that man becomes worse than the first. So shall it be also with this evil generation."

The redactional thread of this chapter has now led from the citation of Isa 42:1–4 forward to the Beelzebul narrative and its fulfillment of the first promise to the Messiah, and to the "sign of Jonah" passage and its fulfillment of the second promise. Both passages have included rather bitter invective against the opponents of Jesus. The chapter is brought to a close by the pericope concerning the desire of the family of Jesus to see him. Does it fit into the structure of the chapter?

81. The seminal idea for this reconstructed source came from a brief remark by Dr. David Flusser in a lecture delivered at Union Theological Seminary, New York, 1966. Evidence for a tripartite expectation: prophet, priest, and king, is extensive in the writings from Qumran. See K. G. Kuhn, "The Two Messiahs of Aaron and Israel," in *The Scrolls and the New Testament*, ed. by K. Stendahl (New York: Harper and Brothers, 1957), 54–64.

The introduction to the pericope has no relation to the context. "While he was still speaking to the people, behold his mother and his brothers stood outside, asking to see him" (12:46). No crowds have been mentioned in the preceding verses.[82] Rather, Jesus has been speaking directly to his opponents. Once again the thread of organization is not that of consecutive narrative.

In each of the preceding major sections of the chapter, it was possible to discern a connection that had been made directly between the Isaiah citation and the Matthean passage. This suggests that a similar clue may explain the position of the pericope about the family of Jesus. Once the problem has been seen in that light, a connection is clear. The opening phrase of the Isaiah citation was conformed to the voice at the baptism (see above, p. 36) except in one important respect. At the baptism the designation for Jesus is unequivocally *son* **(υἱός)**. The word used in 12:18 is the word which can mean either son or servant **(παῖς)**. The adaptation to the baptism words shows that this is a very careful choice. The context of Isa 42:1–4 requires servant, but the words from the baptism remind the reader that **παῖς** can also mean son.[83]

The pericope about the family of Jesus is concerned with a son and his family. That alone would provide no connection to the Isaiah text. The important feature there is "my [i.e., God's] servant/son." Matthew has, therefore, shaped the tradition into a story revealing the fact that Jesus is God's son. This is accomplished through the answer to the family's request: "And stretching his hand to the disciples, he said, 'Here are my mother and my brothers. For whoever does the will of my Father in heaven is my brother and sister and mother.'" The disciples are brothers and sisters, but Jesus is the son of the Father in heaven. Matthew has made the pericope into an affirmation of the designation of the Messiah in 12:18, "Behold my son/servant whom I have chosen, my beloved with whom my soul is well pleased." The two promises to the Messiah: possession of the Spirit and pronouncing judgment to the Gentiles, are both fulfilled in Jesus, the beloved servant/son.

A retracing of the redactional thread by which Matthew has organized ch. 12 indicates that the Isaiah citation has played a decisive role. The withdrawal of Jesus from public ministry in view of the hostility of the Pharisees prompted the formula citation. From the citation, lines of connection were then drawn to the Beelzebul controversy in which the possession of the Spirit by Jesus was affirmed, to the "sign of Jonah" pericope in which the promise to "proclaim justice to the Gentiles" was affirmed in Jesus, and to the "family of Jesus" pericope in which it was shown that Jesus was the

82. Neither is this introduction exactly paralleled in Mk or Lk, although Lk 8:19 does mention the crowd.

83. The appropriate use of **παῖς** is noted by W. C. Allen, *The Gospel According to St. Matthew* (3rd ed., Edinburgh: T. & T. Clark, 1912), 130–131.

son/servant of the citation. In all three cases it is apparent that there are no other connections between the passages and that there is, indeed, some disjuncture between each section and its preceding context.

Matthew has taken separate words, or ideas, from the citation and illustrated them in the material of 12:22–50. This type of arrangement is keyword (German, *Stichwort*) exegesis and was a fairly common practice in first-century Jewish literature. For example, many of the Tannaitic Midrashim passages are collections of various traditions which relate to the words of the OT text under discussion only by attachment to individual words of the text. In the *Mekilta of R. Ishmael,* a second-century document which takes up many older traditions, this type of organization is very common. Series of comments are made about the word "saying" in Ex 12:1, the pronoun "this" in Ex 12:2, and the right and left hands mentioned in Lev 14:22–52.[84] Moreover, a primary technique of the Rabbinic "Y" or halakic homilies was the connection of halakic traditions to the Torah text by means of keyword connection.[85] It is important to note that this technique is quite different from the linear rationale of the Qumran pesher. By using both methods Matthew shows himself to be a flexible and ingenious interpreter of Scripture.

THE ANALYSIS AND THE CONTROLS

The linear analysis has covered the whole of ch. 12. The controls have been employed throughout but now they should be discussed specifically to test the validity of the analysis.

The presence of a discernible and cogent logical pattern was of as great importance for this analysis as for the preceding one. The logical structure which the analysis reveals in the answer of Jesus to the charge of the Pharisees (25–37) is a defense of the method in itself. The evidence that the author is able to tie together so many elements, often diverse bits of tradition, into one sustained argument is important because it is internally defensible. In the same way, the application of this control makes the redactional connections in the story about the return of the unclean spirit (43–45) very probable. In a negative way, the absence of logical pattern was helpful for the identification of possible traditional material because there was no discernible pattern of Matthean logic connecting the Jonah and queen of the South passages (41–42) and further examination revealed a

84. *Mekilta de Rabbi Ishmael,* trans. by J. Z. Lauterbach (Philadelphia: Jewish Publication Society of America, 1933), I, 1–54.

85. J. Mann, *The Bible as Read and Preached in the Old Synagogue.* II (Cincinnati: Hebrew Union College, 1966), especially "Prolegemena," 1–21. The "Y" is for the first word of the homilies which cites the halakah, "yelammedenu" (and they taught).

possible non-Matthean traditional connection. A further negative application of the control of logical pattern was the evidence at three points that the transitions from pericope to pericope were not by logical, straight-forward narration (the transitions were: from the citation text to the Beelzebul controversy, from that controversy to the "sign of Jonah" pericope, and from the return of the unclean spirit to the family of Jesus pericope). That information led to the consideration of the role of the OT citation in the structure of the passage.

Evidence for the use of the OT source as a controlling feature was gathered with relation to the Isa 42:1–4 citation. The only connections that could be seen between the Beelzebul controversy, the sign of Jonah question, and the family of Jesus pericope were by a direct linking of each to some portion of the Isaiah text. The Beelzebul controversy was related to the first, and the "sign of Jonah" question to the second of the promises to the Messiah that are made in the text. The family of Jesus pericope is a "proof" of the designation of Jesus as son/servant. The value of this evidence lies in the way in which these clues to the structural organization of the passage also opened the way to clues to the internal construction of the pericopes.

Helpful clues in establishing the work of Matthew by way of characteristics and motifs were the following:

17 the citation formula is characteristic of other Matthean citations.
18 the use in the citation of the words from the voice at the baptism, 3:17.
33 a repetition in a similar but unrelated context of the tree and its fruits analogy, 7:17–18 //12:33.
38 Matthew's strong interest in the Pharisees as opponents recurs in 12:14,24 and 38.
45 Matthew's preoccupation with this evil generation (9 times in the gospel, 4 in this passage) is a clue to his work.
50 the use of "my Father in heaven" in the pronouncement about Jesus' sonship combines a Matthean characteristic with the internal logic of the redaction.

All these Matthean characteristics establish the flow of Matthew's thought. And these characteristics are buttressed by the use of the other controls.

This analysis, therefore, lends strong support to the view that it is the author of the gospel who constructed this passage in this precise way. At no point does the logical structure of a pericope defy the connection to the OT text which has been proposed. At no point do the Matthean characteristics go against the grain of either the logical patterns or the connections to the citation. There is strong internal evidence that Matthew has organized 12:1–50 around the Isaiah citation and that vss. 22–50 consist of material designed to support Jesus' messiahship as it is presented in Isa 42:1–4.

THE ANALYSIS AND THE SYNOPTIC PROBLEM

The fact that all of the material in Mt 12:1–50 is paralleled in Mark or Luke except the citation text in 12:17–21 points to a complex set of literary relationships. It is only in the Beelzebul controversy, 12:22–37, that the linear analysis may bring some new evidence to light.

It has long been recognized that Matthew and Luke are closer to each other in this passage than either is to Mark. The most common solution to this puzzle has been the view that Matthew and Luke had a Q version of the story available to them as well as the Marcan one.[86]

Two features of the linear analysis deserve further attention in the source critical discussion of the passage. First, if the analysis is correct, Matthew's development of the controversy depends very much upon an element external to the debate itself; that is, the promise of the spirit to the Messiah in the Isaiah text. Second, Matthew builds a tight logical argument demonstrating that Jesus possesses the Spirit. This new evidence of redactional structure raises the question, as in the previous analysis, of the possible importance of the overlapping of redactional motif from one text to another. Some elements of the Matthean argument are present in Mark (the Spirit and blasphemy sayings, 3:28–30) and in Luke (the "your sons" argument in 11:18–20 and the blasphemy saying in 12:10) but are not integral parts of their arguments. Further work is needed on the redactional structure of the parallel passages before this evidence can be properly assessed.[87]

THE ANALYSIS AND FORM CRITICISM

Although the linear analysis of Mt 12:1–50 does suggest some specific corrections in the form critical tradition about these passages, it does not in any way seriously challenge the principles of form critical analysis. Indeed, in the case of the "something greater than . . . is here" sayings, it seems likely that a new form of logion has been discovered (above, p. 43f.). Formal

86. Bultmann, *History of the Synoptic Tradition,* 13–14, gives a good brief treatment of the relationships. He also attempts a linear reading of Mk's passage. An article by B. S. Easton, "The Beezebul Actions," *JBL* 32 (1913) 57–73, illustrates the more piecemeal approach of the early literary critics and the lack of attention to redactional structure in the accounts.

87. H. G. Wood, "The Priority of Mark," *ExpT 65* (1953–54), 17–19, suggests that Mk's structure may be chiastic. The elements of the chiasmus are a) Jesus' family seeks him because they think he is insane, b) the Pharisees make the same charge, "He has Beelzebul," b') Jesus accuses the Pharisees of blasphemy for their charge, and a') the family is rebuked also. All of this may be true. Wood thought that this proved Marcan priority because that structure is broken in Mt and Lk. However, it is striking that none of the Marcan elements which produce the chiasmus are present in either Mt or Lk, nor are the Marcan chiastic elements germane to the content of the material. Jesus' sanity is not in question in the Beelzebul controversy or in the pericope about Jesus' family except in Mk's version. Wood does not establish Mk's priority here but he may have the clue to Marcan redaction.

analysis assisted the redaction analysis in outlining the Beelzebul controversy. Some of the elements of that controversy, notably the "Spirit of God" saying in vss. 27–28 and the "blasphemy" saying in vss. 31–32, may not be as easily separated from the context as independent sayings in light of the redactional logic that has been found in Matthew's Beelzebul controversy, but on the whole the formal patterns are consistent with prior views of the material. There does not appear to be any point in the chapter where a form critical principle is so important as to force a revision of the proposed redactional thread.

THE ANALYSIS AND AN UNDERSTANDING OF MATTHEW

The progress in perceiving the craft of Matthew which has been made by the linear analysis of Mt 12:1–50 is extensive. It is possible to categorize the redactional insights gained as 1) further evidence of the author's skill in using the OT, 2) important evidence concerning the author's Messianic theology, and 3) further evidence of the Jewish-Christian situation which the author's work presupposes.

In the parables discourse the author developed a theory of interpreting the parables and then rigorously applied the theory in the three interpretations of the chapter. In the process the OT texts were treated differently. Isa 6:9–10 was used in an allusive way with the main words of that allusion becoming the key words for the interpretation of the parable of the Sower. Ps 78:2 was fully cited and was treated as a thematic restatement of the theory of parable.

In 12:18–21, the author has used a citation text which he has freely shaped to suit his own purposes in applying the servant text to Jesus (above, pp. 34ff.). The freedom of the citation, especially in the incorporation of a part of the baptism announcement (vs. 18b), makes it possible for critics to call the technique Targumizing.[88] Whatever one chooses to call the technique, it is important to recognize that the freedom exhibited by Matthew in citing the text is controlled by his purposes in the construction of the gospel. It would hardly be correct to call such a use of the OT irreverent. Matthew simply uses the text in such a way as to make clear to the reader its application to Jesus. In this shaping of the text, he again testifies to his belief that the OT, and especially the prophets, point forward to Jesus and the coming of the kingdom.

The most valuable result of the linear analysis for Matthew's use of the OT does not concern the citation itself but the connections which have been drawn from the citation to the rest of the chapter. The keyword or theme

88. R. Gundry, *The Use of the Old Testament in St. Matthew's Gospel,* 172ff., prefers this term for Mt's citation technique. Stendahl also uses this term for the Isaiah citation in 12:18–21 (*School,* 115).

method of connection (by which the Beelzebul controversy, the sign of Jonah pericope, and the family of Jesus pericope were related to the Isaiah citation) was most closely paralleled in the midrashic tradition of Judaism (above, p. 46). That it occurred to the author to buttress his application of Isa 42:1–4 to Jesus by means of separate passages connecting key words or ideas from the text to the pericopes is firm evidence that the writer is one trained in the use of the OT for just such purposes.[89] This is more than Targumic adaptation of the text to fit Jesus. It is also a clever application of the text to parts of the tradition about Jesus. The evidence gathered here should alert the reader of Matthew to the possibility that other similar types of connection between portions of the gospel and OT citations and allusions may exist.

The keyword application of Isa 42:1–4, as well as the form of the citation, reveals an important aspect of Matthew's view of Jesus. The main feature of this chapter is its strong attention to the theme that Jesus is the servant/ Messiah. Even the traditional Son of David title (12:23) is taken up under the overall picture of Jesus as the fulfillment of the Servant prophecy. The evidence from the Targum to Isaiah forbids any claim that this identification is Matthew's own idea or even a uniquely Christian one (above, p. 36). It is evident, from Matthew's careful application of the theme to Jesus, that Matthew believes that Jesus is a fulfillment of this Messianic promise. Moreover, the fulfillment in Jesus need not yet be completed. Matthew's vision of the role of Jesus encompasses not only his life and death and present Lordship over the church but also the work of the Messiah in judgment (this is apparent in the application of the Jonah pericope to the Isaiah text, see above, p. 42f.). The main theme of 12:18–50 is the affirmation that Jesus is the servant Messiah. That theme is portrayed by means of a series of pictures in which people: the Pharisees, the scribes, this evil generation, and even the family of Jesus, fail to see who Jesus is.

The failure of people to recognize Jesus as the servant Messiah is illustrated by Matthew primarily as a conflict between Jesus and the Pharisees: the Pharisees react to his Sabbath activities by a plot (vss. 13–14), they charge that his exorcisms are done by the power of Beelzebul (vs. 24), and they seek a sign (vs. 38). It is possible that Matthew is responsible for the presence of the Pharisees in both of the latter instances. In any case, the chapter reveals the conflict of Jesus and the Pharisees which is an important feature of the gospel as a whole. This is important for a redactional appraisal of Matthew because it shows that 1) in passages where intense controversy with Jesus occurs and 2) in controversies that are inherently of a Jewish vs. Christian nature (Beelzebul and the request for a sign) Matthew makes the

89. This is in full accord with the position of Gärtner that the situation for the effort to provide OT bases for Messianic claims about Jesus was the mission to the Jews (Gärtner, "The Habbakuk Commentary and the Gospel of Matthew," 22–24).

opponents the Pharisees. It is apparent that both the Beelzebul charge and the request for a sign were of great interest to Matthew because he presents doublets of the initial portions of each passage.[90] In both passages in ch. 12 the shape of the pericopes did not come from a source taken over by Matthew but it was produced by the author himself. All of this suggests that Matthew is a Jewish-Christian for whom the Pharisees are *the principal* Jewish opponents and these opponents call Christian exorcisms demonically inspired and deny that there is scriptural evidence for the Messiahship of Jesus.

This conclusion supports the view of R. Hummel with regard to the Jewish-Christian vs. Pharisaic Jewish debate that comes to the surface in Matthew.[91] The separation of the church from the synagogue is a painful factor in Matthew's situation and the conflict for the loyalties of Jewish people is a live one. This means that the situation in which Matthew wrote was probably not a time when the separation of Christianity from Judaism was complete and final.[92] It is more likely that Matthew reflects the tensions of the time after 70 A.D. when Pharisaism struggled for control over the remnant Judaism and when Christianity was finally expelled from the Jewish community by means of the Benediction against the heretics.[93] That

90. A third use of the Beelzebul charge in 10:25 makes it quite clear that the Beelzebul charge is not just a bygone matter but a point of conflict in Mt's day, "If they have called the master of the house Beelzebul, how much more will they malign those of his household."

91. Hummel seeks to show how this conflict is determinative for much of Matthew, especially the *Streitgespräche* (*Die Auseinandersetzung,* 34–71).

92. Both Trilling, *Das wahre Israel,* and D. R. A. Hare, *The Theme of Jewish Persecution in the Gospel according to St. Matthew* (Cambridge: Cambridge University Press, 1967), have argued for this full and complete separation, and there is some evidence to support their views. Mt 21:43, "Therefore I tell you, the kingdom of God will be taken away from you and given to a nation producing the fruits of it." This verse can certainly be read as a final concession of the failure of the mission to Israel and a turning to the Gentiles as a result. The mission pronouncement of 28:16–20 may also be cited in support of this view. A thorough acceptance of this position, however, requires the assignment of a great deal of material to a source used by the author which had the sort of Jewish-Christian outlook described in the linear analysis. Moreover, it has already been noted that the universalistic outlook of 28:16–20 should almost certainly be tempered by the kind of salvation history view present in 24:14. That Mt can be less than precise in making these distinctions may be seen in the statement in 8:12, "while the sons of the kingdom will be thrown into the outer darkness," which compares the faith of the centurion to that of Israel. One would hardly expect the "sons of the kingdom" to mean just Israelites, as it must here, if the use of the same term in the parable interpretation of 13:37ff. is kept in mind. This evidence suggests that Mt thinks best in terms of Israel against the world but that the fact of the rejection of the messiahship of Jesus by the Pharisees has forced him to alter his view and to formulate a picture of a different "true Israel." The important insights of Trilling and Hare need to be incorporated into a more complex picture of the relationship of Mt to Judaism by utilizing Hummel's results and the evidence gathered by these linear analyses.

93. The alteration of the 18 Benedictions to include a curse of the Nazarenes and heretics was made under Gamaliel the Second, head of the Jamnia academy from c. 85–115 A.D. Its end result was the separation of church and synagogue completely. See the discussion of the *Birkath ha Minim* given by J. L. Martyn in *History and Theology in the Fourth Gospel,* 31–41. Hummel

is as close as the evidence of the linear analysis of Mt 12:1–50 allows the placing of the situation of Matthew because no mention is made of further details of the conflict. This evidence needs to be considered, however, with the other elements in Matthew which deal with the tension of church and synagogue in the search for a firm statement of the Matthean situation.

The linear analysis of Mt 12:1–50 has supported the hypothesis that the author of the gospel uses the OT citations to shape the material around them. Matthew employed a special Messianic interpretation of Isa 42:1–4 as the basis of an extended treatment of the charge that Jesus acts in his exorcisms by the power of Beelzebul. The whole of the section 12:22–50 has been shown to reflect Jewish-Christian concerns and motifs. Matthew has employed elements from the tradition available to him in ways that suit his own special purposes. This is especially evident in the application of the Jonah pericope to the promise of the servant's proclamation of justice to the Gentiles, and in Matthew's use of the pericope about the family of Jesus to affirm Jesus' sonship. The interest shown in the struggle with the Pharisees over specific problems of tension between Jewish-Christians and Pharisaic Jews, namely, the Beelzebul charge and the request for a sign, helps to illumine the situation of Matthew in relationship to Judaism. This analysis has thus achieved much in the search for a picture of Matthew and his work.

ANALYSIS 3: MT 15:1-20 AND ISA 29:13

A third passage in which an OT citation may play an important structural role is the clean/unclean debate in Mt 15:1–20. A citation occurs in the midst of the passage, 15:8, which may help to shape the structure of the Matthean version of the debate. A second clue to Matthean exegetical work occurs immediately after the citation.

> And he called the people to him and said to them,
> "Hear and understand" (15:10).

It has already been shown that such calls to hearing in Mt 13 (vss. 9, 18, and 43) are calls to exegetical perception. Therefore, Mt 15:1–20 is a passage where the hypothesis of Matthean structural use of the OT may be tested. The passage may be outlined as follows:

- 1–2 An introductory challenge by Pharisees and scribes criticizing the disciples' failure to wash their hands when they eat.
- 3–6 A counterquestion asked by Jesus concerning the allowance of dedicatory (Qorban) vows by the Pharisees.

---

argues (*Die Auseinandersetzung,* 28–33) with good reason that the positive relationships of Matthew to Judaism (see 23:1–2) would not be possible after the change in the Benedictions and that Mt must predate the enactment of the curse against the Christians and heretics. If this can be supported, it is an important item for dating and locating Mt in early Christian history.

7–9 The citation of Isa 29:13.
10–11 A brief explanatory statement for the people.
12–20 A more complete explanation of the explanatory statement for the disciples.

A preliminary form critical analysis is difficult in this case. However, the following components may tentatively be suggested. 1) the opening section, vss. 1–6, constitutes a *question-counterquestion* controversy. The form is the same as that in the controversies which open ch. 12 (12:1–8 and 9–13).[94] The second block of material is the formula citation. After this it is difficult to describe the blocks which make up the passage. Vs. 10 is a call to assent. Vs. 11 is an enigmatic logion apparently complete in itself. Vss. 12–14 deal with an objection by the Pharisees that is reported to Jesus by the disciples. Vss. 13–14 give Jesus' reply against the Pharisees by means of two analogies; the unsound tree and the blind guides. In vss. 15–20 an explanation of the logion in vs. 11 is given to the disciples. These verses do not form a distinct unit but are dependent upon the context and upon vs. 11 for their structure and logic.

THE LINEAR ANALYSIS OF MT 15:1–20

The introductory verse of the passage begins with a Matthean *then* (τότε) and is entirely unrelated to the preceding portion of ch. 14. The *then* marks a new turn of thought. Since 15:1–20 also prove to be unrelated to the pericope which follows, it is possible that the passage is an insertion into a source which proceeded directly from 14:36, which is set at Gennesaret, to 15:21, in which Jesus withdraws to Tyre and Sidon. Though attractive, this possibility cannot be firmly established.[95] It is clear, however, that 15:1–20 has no logical connection to the preceding or to the following material.

The interlocutors of Jesus are Pharisees and scribes from Jerusalem. In this instance the Pharisees are germane to the context (see below on 15:2), and their presence here cannot be due to Matthew. The question they address to Jesus is, "Why do your disciples transgress the traditions of the elders? For they do not wash their hands when they eat." This is a direct question about the failure of Jesus and the disciples[96] to follow a long-

94. For other New Testament and numerous Rabbinic examples of the form see Bultmann, *History of the Synoptic Tradition,* 41–45. It should be noted that Bultmann beginning from Mk's (41) form, classes this pericope differently.

95. It is worth noting here that exactly the same order and lack of connection occur in the Marcan parallel so that the same suggestion is in order there in terms of the placing of this pericope.

96. On the tendency of the tradition to place the burden of criticism on the disciples rather than Jesus directly see Bultmann, *History of the Synoptic Tradition,* 44–49.

established Pharisaic custom. It was not an OT law that was in question but a purification ritual which had grown up in the oral tradition.[97]

The reply of Jesus is not in the form of an excuse or a denial of the charge. Instead, it takes the form of a counterquestion challenging the validity of the oral tradition on which the handwashing rule depends. Since neither here nor anywhere is the original charge denied, it is safe to assume that at whatever stage in the tradition the pericope was formed, the charge was accurate.

The counterquestion 15:3–6 is:

> He answered them, "And why do you transgress the commandment of God for the sake of your tradition? For God commanded, 'Honor your father and your mother,' and, 'He who speaks evil of father or mother, let him surely die.' But you say, 'If any one tells his father or his mother, "What you would have gained from me is given to God," he need not honor his father.' So, for the sake of your tradition, you have made void the law of God."

This counterquestion has been much discussed. It contains no distinctively Matthean features. The matter of dedicatory vows was seriously debated in Pharisaic Judaism in the era of 70–135 A.D.[98] It is quite possible that the custom of disinheriting parents by means of a dedicatory vow was older than 70. Therefore, the origin of the pericope cannot be exactly fixed.[99] The most distinctive feature of the argument is the same use of the Decalogue to challenge the oral tradition. While the validity of such an argument in first-century Judaism may be debated,[100] it is clear that a tendency of the Synoptic controversy stories is the support of the countering thrust by OT texts.[101]

For an understanding of the Matthean version of the debate, the questions of origin and intent in the Qorban controversy are less important than the question of how this passage provides a suitable preface for the citation of Isa 29:13. It is cited 15:7ff. in the following way:

97. A full discussion of the traditional rule and the debate among the Rabbis over whether it was exegetically or traditionally based, is given in Strack-Billerbeck, *Kommentar,* I, 695–704.

98. V. Taylor, *Mark,* 341–342.

99. J. Fitzmyer, "The Aramaic Qorban Inscription from Jebel Hallet Et-Turi and Mk 7:11/Mt. 15:5," *JBL* 78 (1959), 60–65, argues that the evidence of a first-century tomb inscription which speaks of the Qorban custom means that the custom was common before 70. Also, G. W. Buchanan, "Some Vow and Oath Formulas in the New Testament," *HTR* 58 (1965) 319-326, has presented a firm argument that the Qorban retort may rest on a "minced oath formula." His view that 15:4-5 is an expansion of an original *chreia* preserved in 1–3 is not convincing. 15:3 is not an adequate retort to the Pharisees' question. That the Pharisees transgress the law of God has to be demonstrated for the charge to be decisive. The necessary demonstration is the use of Qorban (vss. 4–5).

100. C. G. Montefiore roundly condemns this use of the Decalogue against the oral law, while most Christian scholars defend it. See Montefiore, *The Synoptic Gospels,* I (2nd ed., revised; New York: Macmillan, 1927), 164ff.

101. Bultmann, *History of the Synoptic Tradition,* 41, gives a list of Synoptic examples and on p. 45, Rabbinic examples.

> You hypocrites! Well did Isaiah prophesy of you, when he said, "This people honors me with their lips, but their heart is far from me; in vain they worship me, teaching as doctrines the precepts of men."

In order to grasp the connection between this text and the Qorban retort, it is necessary to observe some features of the text itself.

Isa 29:13 is not given as a standard Matthean formula citation. The regular form of such a citation is, "This was to fulfill what was spoken by the prophet Isaiah" (cf. 12:17). This particular citation is, however, the only non-citation formula in the tradition which is spoken by Jesus (excluding Mt 13:14–15, for the reasons noted above in Analysis 1). In fact, only one other non-formula text in Matthew names the prophet, Mt 3:3, and that may well be in a pre-Matthean tradition. There is, therefore, a good reason to examine this introduction. Since the phrase "you hypocrites" is such a favorite description of the Pharisees in Matthew (13 times in Mt, only here in Mk), it is at least possible that the hand of Matthew has shaped this introduction.[102]

The text itself is predominantly that of the LXX. This is so important a point that the texts of the relevant LXX forms and the MT will be cited so that the reader may grasp the data. The form of the citation presents two problems which bear directly on Matthew's application of the Isaiah text.

THE TEXT FORMS OF ISA 29:13

LXX	Matthew	Hebrew
καὶ εἶπεν κύριος		ויאמר אדני יען כי
Ἐγγίζει μοι ὁ λαὸς	*ὁ λαὸς*	נגש העם הזה בפיו
οὗτος[103] *τοῖς χείλεσιν*	*οὗτος τοῖς χείλεσίν*	
αὐτῶν τιμῶσίν με	*με τιμᾷ*	ובשפתיו כבדוני
ἡ δὲ καρδία αὐτῶν	*ἡ δὲ καρδία αὐτῶν*	
πόρρω ἀπέχει ἀπ'	*πόρρω ἀπέχει ἀπ'*	ולבו רחק ממני
ἐμοῦ μάτην δὲ	*ἐμοῦ μάτην δὲ*	
σέβονταί με	*σέβονταί με*	[104]ותהי יראתם אתי

102. The assumption that Mt took over the text and introduction from Mk has meant that no attention has been paid to the form of this introduction in the recent studies on Mt and the OT (Stendahl, *School*, 56–58; Gundry, *The Use of the Old Testament in Matthew's Gospel*, 14–16).

103. LXX^{B} has *ἐν τῷ στόματι αὐτοῦ καὶ ἐν* after *ὁ λαὸς οὗτος*.

104. The Targum reads this clause in the same way as the MT does. The whole clause is the condition for God's threatened action, 29:14: "Therefore, behold, I will again do marvelous things."

LXX	Matthew	Hebrew
διδάσκοντες	διδάσκοντες	
ἐντάλματα ἀνθρώπων	διδασκαλίας	מצות אנשים
καὶ διδασκαλίας	ἐντάλματα ἀνθρώπων	מלמדה

The fundamental similarity between the Matthean text form and the LXX is evident in the structure of the passage. The fact that not only Matthew and Mark, but also the forms found in I Clement 15:2 and Justin Martyr, *Dialogue with Trypho* 78:11, use the shorter LXX form shows that this was the form known to the early Christian writers.[105] In Matthew the opening sentence is smoothed by using a single predicate. This is possible for the author because the meaning depends primarily upon the LXX rendering of the second major clause, "in vain they worship me," whether or not this LXX rendering rests on a special reading of the Hebrew text or upon the translators' error.[106]

Matthew's form differs from the LXX^{A} form in two ways. The last phrase is slightly altered so that the "teachings" and "commandments" are apposite. This change is insignificant.[107] And in the opening phrase the clumsiness of the LXX^{A} form is corrected by omitting the first of the two finite verbs and using the singular "honors" in agreement with the subject "this people." In all likelihood, therefore, Matthew's form of the LXX did not contain the phrase "with their mouths" which corresponds to the Hebrew בפיו. The importance of this fact will become clear as the analysis proceeds.

The citation of Isa 29:13 is used by Matthew to support Jesus' initial retort. The Pharisees claim to honor God. Even the Qorban vow spoken by a man appears on the surface to be an act of honoring God. But in fact it fails to honor God because it places a teaching of men over a commandment of God. This is so direct and so logical a connection that it must be the one intended by Matthew.

Immediately following the citation, Jesus offers a comment to which he exhorts the audience's *hearing* and *understanding*. Matthew's use of these words in the parables discourse in connection with interpretive comment suggests that a search for a relationship between the preceding text and the comment is in order.

105. The longer LXX^{B} form is widely regarded as a hexaplaric emendation. See Stendhal, *School*, 57.

106. Stendhal, *School*, 58 says, "The line of thought in the quotation is wholly dependent upon the LXX's translation of *μάτην* which must revert to וְתֹהוּ instead of the M.T.'s וַתְּהִי."

107. Both Stendhal, *School*, 58, and Gundry, *The Use of the Old Testament in Matthew*, 15, agree that this change in word order carries no importance for the Matthean meaning of the text.

15:11

> Not what goes into the mouth defiles a man, but what comes out of the mouth, this defiles a man.

Several items in the preceding material appear to be relevant to this comment. 1) The question of eating with unwashed hands is a question of defiling food which is put *into* the mouth. 2) The making of a Qorban vow and thereby violating a commandment of God is a defilement which comes *out of* the mouth of a man. The first, eating with washed hands, may be seen as honoring God by not defiling one's lips, and the second, making a vow which violates a commandment, is an example of the heart's distance from God. Should this line of reasoning prove to be correct, the comment in vs. 11 restates the argument that it is not ritual purification of the mouth which is important, but what is spoken by the mouth. This may indicate that Matthew is aware of the use of mouth in the Hebrew text of Isa 29:13.[108] A contrast is drawn between the eating function of the mouth (or the lips)[109] and the speaking function. That the comment in vs. 11 is exegetically related to the Isaiah text may be stated as a tentative suggestion needing further support.

The next verses deal with the reaction of the Pharisees to Jesus' reply to their question. The disciples report that the Pharisees were scandalized. This is hardly surprising. Jesus' answer has called into serious question the binding validity of the oral Torah, which was a cardinal tenet of Pharisaism.[110] Moreover, it could be considered that the blunt comment of vs. 11 was a total rejection of the laws of clean and unclean.[111] The Pharisees certainly would have been disturbed by either or both of the parts of Jesus' reply.

The response which Jesus makes to the report of the Pharisees' anger is an outburst, vss. 13–14, against the Pharisees themselves:

> Every plant which my heavenly Father has not planted will be rooted up. Let them alone; they are blind guides. And if a blind man leads a blind man, both will fall into a pit.

108. Since it has already been shown that Mt uses both Greek and Hebrew texts (esp. in using Ps 78:2 and Isa 42:1–4, see above), it is not necessary to insist that Mt had the longer LXX version. He could also have used the Hebrew.

109. The speech function of both mouth and lips predominates in biblical usage (Bauer-Arndt-Gingrich, *A Greek-English Lexicon of the New Testament*, 777 and 887) so that Mt's combination of the physiological and speaking functions is quite unique, but logical.

110. The tradition that the oral law goes back to God's delivery of it to Moses on Sinai may be seen in the opening verses of *Pirke Aboth*.

111. Compare the number of rules for defilement in the Pharisaic tradition as given in Appendix LV of Danby's *Mishnah*, 800–804, and the whole sixth division of the *Mishnah*, *Tohoroth*, which is devoted to the subject. There is even a special portion of this division devoted to hands, *Yadaim*. H. Danby, trans., *The Mishnah* (London: Oxford University Press, 1967).

For evidence that Matthew is responsible for this reply the following data may be marshalled: 1) "My heavenly Father" is a characteristic Matthean phrase. 2) The use of the metaphor of the uprooting of intruding plants is exactly the same as the use in the interpretation of the parable of the Tares. 3) "Blind guides" as a designation for the Pharisees occurs again in Mt 23:16-20 and there in connection with the problem of vows, just as here in relation to the Qorban vow. This is more than enough evidence to show that Matthew has compiled these verses as a means of attacking the Pharisaic opponents because of their displeasure with the reply to their question.

Peter persists: "Explain the parable to us." It is difficult at first glance to see a referent for this request. No parable has been spoken here. The two analogies just applied to the Pharisees are hardly difficult enough to need explanation. Since, however, the word parable had the broad meaning of figurative speech, the reader's attention is directed toward the enigmatic logion of vs. 11.

Jesus asks Peter, "Are you still without understanding?" These words are reminiscent of the attempt that was made in the parables discourse to teach the disciples how to interpret the parables and their subsequent assertion that they understand, 13:51. The renewed emphasis on understanding (cf. vs. 10) suggests that an exegetical problem is involved.

Jesus proceeds in vss 17–20 to make the meaning of the logion of vs. 11 clear:

> Do you not see that whatever goes into the mouth passes into the stomach, and so passes on? But what comes out of the mouth proceeds from the heart, and this defiles a man. For out of the heart come evil thoughts, murder, adultery, fornication, theft, false witness, slander. These are what defile a man; but to eat with unwashed hands does not defile a man.

This explanation of vs. 11 adds an important element to that statement, one which is essential to it. In vs. 11 the contrast is between "what goes into the mouth" and "what comes out of the mouth." As a consequence, the physiological functions of the mouth are brought into the discussion. It is fairly clear from the context and from a common sense application that "what goes into the mouth" is intended to be food and drink. However, it is not at all clear just what "comes out of the mouth" may mean. For example, both breath and spittle can come from the mouth. Does Mt 15:11 mean that these things defile a man? In view of this ambiguity, a further explanation is needed. "That which goes into the stomach and so passes on" confirms the view that "what goes into the mouth" means food and drink. But, "That which comes out of the mouth proceeds from the heart, and this defiles a man" makes it equally clear that "what comes out of the mouth" refers only to speech. The essential qualifying phrase is "from the heart" (cf. Mt 12:34b). The contrast intended is between food which is taken into the mouth and words which come from the heart.

But why is the contrast put in just these terms? A glance back to the Isaiah text reveals both the contrast and the terms:

> This people honors me with their lips, but their heart is far from me (vs. 8).

The presence of the qualifying phrase, "from the heart," in the Matthean explanation (vs. 18) confirms the suggestion made above that the original saying is an exegetical comment. The two major terms of the first portion of the Isaiah text, "lips" (syn. mouth) and "heart," are used as the crux of a special argument which justifies the Christian practice of breaking the Pharisaic handwashing regulations. The importance of mouth and heart for this explanation, accompanied by the necessity for a further explanation of vs. 11 to clarify how the heart affects the mouth, proves that the material following the Isaiah citation is related to the question of handwashing by means of key concepts from the Isaiah text. Just as the initial citation of the text depends on a special reading of that text so that handwashing rules are "honoring God with the lips" while the Qorban vow, breaking God's commandment, reveals the intention of the heart, so in the subsequent interpretation the same point is made through reference to the physical organs and their functions. The most important feature is that in this argument it is possible to follow the work of Matthew through his use of the keywords from the Isaiah text.

Two questions remain. Why, if Matthew intended this interpretation, did he not use *lips* instead of *mouth*? Or else, why did Matthew not cite the Hebrew text in order to have the word *mouth* in his text? This question cannot be answered by claiming that Matthew simply copied the text. His freedom in forming a citation to suit his own purposes is readily evident in the Isaiah citation in 12:18–21. Instead, the answer lies in the role the citation plays as a middle term. The logic which called the citation forth depends upon the LXX reading of the text, "In vain they worship me, teaching as doctrines the precepts of men." That accounts for the LXX form of the citation.

When the citation is explained to the disciples, however, the line of interpretation turns on the parts of the body, *mouth* and *heart*, more than on the verbal ideas *honor* and *worship*. The use of the term *mouth* instead of lips is easily understandable for two reasons. It is the more common term for the part of man which speaks (6 times elsewhere in Mt but *lips* only in the citation of 15:8), and it is present in the Hebrew text of Isa 29:13 which was probably known to Matthew. Indeed, the similar contrast drawn in Mt 12:34b, "For out of the abundance of the heart the mouth speaks," may mean that Matthew knew this contrast originally as exegetically related to the Hebrew of Isa 29:13. At any rate, since the logic of the exegesis is precise, and since the reference to the heart in the explanation points *only* to the cited text, it is difficult to claim that the author would have recognized any difficulty in the shift from *lips* to *mouth*. Both words are in the OT text tradition. They are synonyms. *Lips* happen to occur in the text in the way most useful for the initial citation. *Mouth* is the more common term and is used in the explanation which follows. Both the short explanation of the text in vs. 11 and the longer explanation in vss. 16–20 are exegetically related to Isa 29:13.

In the longer explanation, vss. 16–20, further indication of adaptation in the light of the text is apparent in the list of sins. Not all of the sins are verbal sins (murder, adultery, fornication, and theft are not). But evil thoughts, false witness, and slander are verbal sins, and the list begins and ends with one of these. Though the list is a traditional one, it is clearly weighted toward verbal sins in line with the context in which it occurs.

The linear analysis has revealed a special structure in the Matthean version of the debate about clean and unclean. The question of the Pharisaic opponents is met by a counterquestion on the use of Qorban by the Pharisees. This leads to the citation of Isa 29:13. After the citation is completed, an initial exegesis is offered to the crowd. The Pharisees' anger at the reply is dismissed by a Matthean construction which castigates the Pharisees. Then, in response to Peter's further question, the full explanation of the initial exegetical comment is given. The terms of this explanation and the nature of the contrast itself (*into the mouth* and *out of the mouth from the heart*) are drawn from the Isaiah text. The analysis leads to the suggestion, therefore, that vss. 1–6, the question and counterquestion, come to Matthew from the tradition. Vss. 10–20 are arranged and, for the most part, constructed by Matthew to express his particular understanding of the question of handwashing.

This reconstruction of the passage receives support from a closer study of the materials. W. G. Kümmel has noted that the Qorban counterquestion is the substantive answer that is given to the Pharisees' question about handwashing. He argues that this may well have been the original tradition.[112] Two factors strongly favor this hypothesis.

The statement about Qorban is incomplete in and of itself. It is a retort of a rebuke. This retort fits exactly the reply that is needed to the question of the Pharisees about handwashing. The retort deals, as the question does, with the validity of the oral Torah. Such a question and retort has a natural life setting either in the ministry of Jesus or in the conversations of the early Jewish-Christian community with Pharisaic Judaism.

On the other hand, the application of Isa 29:13 to this controversy is entirely dependent upon the LXX form of the text ("in vain they worship me, teaching as doctrines the precepts of men") and must stem from a Greek-speaking church community and must be secondary to the original debate. The tradition behind the Matthean version of the story was very probably a controversy story which consisted of the question of the Pharisees (Mt 15:2) followed by the Qorban retort (Mt 15:3–6).

112. W. G. Kümmel, "Jesus und der jüdische Traditionsgedanke," *ZNW* 33 (1934), 122–123.

Whether the citation, vss. 8–9, is traditional or Matthean is more difficult to judge. While some elements point to Matthean construction (the favorite term "hypocrites" and the mid-term role played by the OT text), others do not (the complete LXX form of the text reveals no Matthean reshaping, and the citation is not strictly a fulfillment citation). Because of this ambiguity, the citation of Isa 29:13 cannot be assigned with certainty either to Matthew or to his tradition.

From the words of vs. 10, "And he called the people to him and said to them, 'Hear and understand,'" through the rest of the passage, Matthew's work is evident. Only in vss 12–14, where comments about the Pharisees which appear to be stock Matthean reprobations are used, is the use of tradition evident. The cursory explanation to the crowds which follows the call to assent is constructed by the use of the key term *mouth* from the Isaiah text. The final, fuller explanation to the disciples, vss. 16–20, makes the connection to the OT text even more precise with the addition of the phrase, "from the heart," in vs. 18. Weighty evidence to the contrary would be necessary to negate the conclusion that vss. 10–20, including vs. 11, were constructed by Matthew.

THE ANALYSIS AND THE CONTROLS

The application of the controls for redaction is made easier by the prior work on chs. 12 and 13. When elements of redactional technique that were discovered in those portions are also identifiable in this analysis, the strength of the analysis is correspondingly greater.

The use of a logical pattern is very important as a control for this analysis. It bears most particularly on the relationship of the initial explanation in vs. 11 to the fuller explanation in vss. 16–20. It was shown that the initial explanation was logically inadequate without the further explication given in the latter passage. The addition of the contrast of the activity of eating with that of speaking from the heart keeps the explanation from dangers of logical absurdity. In the context of Jewish law about clean and unclean, the logion in 15:11 is too vague to be defensible. The logic of the whole passage is required for that verse to be clear and understandable. Furthermore, the steps from question to counterquestion, to citation, to explanation, to anger on the part of the Pharisees, to a rebuttal of them, to a question from the disciples, and to a fuller explanation were all logically traceable. There is a demonstrable logical cohesion to Mt 15:1–20.

The most important external control was once again the OT citation and the clearly definable literary relationship between the explanations and that text. An emphasis on *mouth* alone would have been inadequate to demonstrate the connection, but the contrast of the activity of the mouth in eating to that of the mouth in speaking "from the heart" drew the relationship into a literary unit in which the main words of the text were used to produce the desired contrast.

In terms of Matthean traits, or the first control, a number of items have occurred in the 20 verses of this passage. Matthean characteristics discernible in 15:1–20 are:

1) In vs. 7, the use of "hypocrites" to describe the Pharisees.
2) The application of the cited text to the immediate context, i.e., the Qorban controversy.
3) In vs. 10, the use of a call to "hear and understand" reminiscent of 13:9,18,23,43, and 51.
4) In vs. 13, the phrase "my heavenly Father" (cf. 12:50) and the theme of uprooting intruding plants (cf. 13:36–43).
5) In vs. 14, the theme of "blind guides" used with the same meaning of the same opponents and in relation to the same subject as in 23:16ff. Moreover, this attack on the opponents before concluding the argument is similar to that in the Beelzebul controversy, 12:33–35.
6) In vs. 16, another emphasis on "understanding."
7) In vss. 16–20, the theme of the crucial importance of the spoken word, similar to that of 12:33–37.

In addition to these items, another more substantive one may be cited. The use of Isa 29:13 in a structural way, so that it serves as the logical center for the organization of the passage, is the fourth instance of this special application of the texts that has now been discovered in Matthew (the others are Isa 6:9–10 in 13:13,16–17; Ps 78:2 in 13:35, and Isa 42:1–4 in 12:18–21). The cumulative evidence for this mid-term technique as a trait of Matthew's is very strong.

THE ANALYSIS AND THE SYNOPTIC PROBLEM

A number of source critical questions emerge from this analysis of the Matthean handwashing controversy. Since virtually all of the elements of Mt 15:1–20 are paralleled in Mk 7:1–23[113] but the two orders are radically different, the question of dependence is an intriguing one. Some of the problems which bear on the analysis may be listed as avenues for further inquiry.

1. Is the Qorban controversy more likely to have preceded or to have followed the Isaiah citation in the oldest tradition?[114]

2. Do the un-Matthean forms of the introductory formula and the text itself point to Matthew's use of Mark?

113. Only the *ad hominem* retort to Mt 15:12–14 is not in Mk 7, whereas only the explanation of the Jewish law in Mk 7:3–4 is not paralleled in Mt 15.

114. Kümmel, "Jesus und der jüdische Traditionsgedanke," 122–123, argues for the order "handwashing question, Qorban, citation" as the original logical order of this pericope.

3. Could the material in Mk 7:14–23 have been independent tradition unrelated to the Isaiah text, or are these verses dependent upon interpretation of that text even though less directly than the Matthean parallels?

4. Does Mt 15:11, with the additions concerning "the mouth," represent a modification of the more radical logion of Mk 7:15? Or is the Marcan verse a simplification of the Matthean form and is it, instead of radical in relation to the purification laws, physiologically absurd?[115]

Again, the question of what weight may be given to the overlapping of elements of redactional motif from one gospel to another must also be considered. Most of the keys to the Matthean structure (the Isaiah text, the preliminary comment in Mk 7;15, and the fuller explanation in 7:18–23) are present in Mark but they do not appear to influence the organization of the Marcan passage in so direct a way as in Matthew. Evaluation of this new evidence depends upon further study of the Marcan account and further inquiry into the source-critical value of the phenomena of redactional overlap.

THE LINEAR ANALYSIS AND FORM CRITICISM

Unquestionably the most important form-critical result of the linear analysis is the discovery that the question-counterquestion controversy which opens Matthew's version of the passage is formally and logically more suitable than is Mark's question-citation form. For the moment this can only be cited as an example of the mutual relationships between redaction and form critical methods. However, this is the third controversy story encountered in these analyses in which Matthew begins from a traditional controversy and works out his own purposes from it (the other two are the Beelzebul controversy and the pericope about the sign of Jonah). This information has already proved helpful in clarifying the formal character of the Matthean controversies.

In an earlier attempt to discern a pattern in the Mt-Mk passage, D. Daube suggested that a four-part controversy form was being employed which was familiar among the Rabbis and could mean that most of the Marcan passage was authentic to Jesus.[116] The form he suggested is 1) an opponent's

115. Some proponents of the former position are R. Bultmann, *Jesus and the Word*, trans. by L. Smith and E. Lantero (New York: Charles Schribner's Sons, 1958), 76; E. Käsemann, *Exegetische Versuche und Besinnungen*, I (2nd ed., Göttingen: Vandenhoeck and Ruprecht, 1960), 239–246; and V. Taylor, *Mark*, 220–221. However, the corollaries to the Marcan verse have not been considered. Do *all* of the "things which come out of a man" defile him: breath, sweat, and excretion as well as speech? Is the vagueness of the formula the reason why Mk 7:19b is a necessary addition? Could a statement as physiologically ambiguous as Mk 7:15 have served as a credible comment upon Jewish law either in the ministry of Jesus or in the early Jewish-Christian communities?

116. D. Daube, "Public Retort and Private Explanation," in *The New Testament and Rabbinic Judaism* (London: University of London, Athlone Press, 1956), 141–157.

question, 2) a public retort, mysterious if not misleading, 3) a request in private for further explanation by the disciples of the teacher, and 4) a full explanation with the answer clearly expressed.[117] To apply this structure to the Synoptic pericope, Daube is forced to ignore the Qorban retort and the Isaiah citation. He says, "Jesus, after some general reflections on the behavior of his opponents, declares: 'There is nothing from without a man. . . .'"[118] The linear analysis has shown that neither the Qorban retort nor the text cited rank as "general comments" but have important bearing on the structure of the passage. Therefore a modification of Daube's rather rigid application of the form to the Synoptic passage is necessary. Matthew may have employed a public retort–private explanation form (with which he was familiar from his Jewish background) in order to adapt the original handwashing controversy (which utilized the Qorban retort) to his particular interests by means of an exegetical comment consisting of enigmatic public comment (vs. 11) and fuller private explanation to the disciples (vss. 16–20). The original controversy was not so constructed, however, and the latter parts are Matthew's creations and do not go back to Jesus.[119]

THE ANALYSIS AND AN UNDERSTANDING OF MATTHEW

The linear analysis of Matthew 15:1–20 assists us in the search for Matthew's work in a number of ways. It has shown Matthew at work shaping a passage around an OT citation in mid-point fashion just as in chs. 12 and 13. It has given another example of the author's use of the keyword or theme technique in using OT (13:12,16,17 and 12:18–21 as applied by Mt). Certain Matthean characteristics appear within the passage and provide support for the analysis.

A further conflict with the Pharisees also occurs and is largely shaped by Matthew. As in the Beelzebul controversy, the interests of Matthew in defending the activities of the church against the opposition of the Pharisees become evident. In the Beelzebul controversy, Matthew argued that Jesus' exorcisms, far from being demonically inspired, were evidence of the activity of the Holy Spirit at work in Jesus. Matthew's church very likely continued the practice of exorcism, met the same opposition, and argued in Matthew's way that their exorcisms were signs of their possession of the Holy Spirit.[120] In this way, Matthew has dovetailed his account of Jesus' life and the situation of his own day.

The same dovetailing has probably occurred in the handwashing controversy as Matthew shapes it. The tradition Matthew takes up in the

117. Daube, 141.
118. Daube, 142.
119. Against Daube's conclusions, 143.
120. See above, p. 51, footnote 90.

opening question-counterquestion may or may not go back to Jesus. It is, however, quite likely that the handwashing controversy was a live issue between Jewish-Christians who allowed table fellowship with Gentiles and "sinners"[121] and the stricter Pharisees.

There is some indication, however, that Matthew realized the radical nature of the Qorban retort as a rejection of the oral law *in toto* and wanted to limit the discussion solely to the handwashing question. This would explain why the contrast of "law of God vs. laws of men" from the Qorban retort is not taken up in the exegesis of the text, but instead the precise and limited contrast is between eating and speaking. By this Matthew means to reject only this aspect of the oral tradition and not the whole.

As G. Barth says,

> Matthew scarcely bases his rejection of the washing of hands on the rejection of the Rabbinic tradition, for elsewhere he impartially adopts tenets from the Rabbinic tradition or appeals to them. The interpretation of the law is rather for him the deciding criterion. In 23:23, where the extension of tithing to spices is a Rabbinic amplification of the law, he adopts the Rabbinic tradition.[122]

Hummel also has argued that Matthew does not intend here to abrogate the entire oral tradition but only this one halakah.[123] Matthew takes a positive as well as negative stance toward the Pharisaic tradition (cf. 23:2f). He is not willing to treat radically the implications of 15:6, "So, for the sake of your tradition, you have made void the law of God." Wherever the Rabbinic tradition is in accord with the will of God as Matthew understands Jesus to have revealed it, there the tradition will be honored; but where it conflicts with God's will, it will be opposed.

This linear analysis has traced the work of Matthew through 15:1–20. The proposed analysis meets the criteria of the controls. It adds new data for both source and form questions. Most important, it provides further evidence about Matthew having been a Jewish-Christian, writing for a Jewish-Christian community which was in live controversy with Pharisaic Judaism.

ANALYSIS 4: MT 9:10–34 AND HOS 6:6

The preceding analyses have brought to light a technique which Matthew employs in constructing his gospel. It is the use of OT texts, through both citation and allusion, to provide the logical framework for the passages in which they occur. Therefore, a search for other such relationships in Matthew is one avenue open for further exploration.

121. Compare Mt 11:19 as a defense of open table fellowship, also 9:10–13.

122. G. Barth in *Tradition and Interpretation in Matthew,* 88.

123. R. Hummel, *Die Auseinandersetzung,* 46–49.

A citation of the OT that may be related to its context is Hos 6:6 in Mt 9:13. The organization of the material following the citation, 9:14–34, diverges sharply from that of either Mark or Luke (where Mk and Lk are closely parallel). This means that Matthew is probably responsible for the structure on *any* source theory. Also, the Hosea text is unique to Matthew. Is it possible that in the construction of the passage Matthew consciously used the citation for a framework?

Mt 9:10–34 may be outlined in the following way:

10–13	The Pharisees question open fellowship and Jesus responds.
(13a)	A citation of Hos 6:6
14–17	The question of fasting.
18–26	The raising of the ruler's daughter.
(20–22)	The incident with the woman who suffered from a hemorrhage.
27–31	Jesus heals two blind men.
32–34	Jesus heals a dumb demoniac.

A preliminary form-critical analysis shows that the passage consists of two controversy stories and four miracle stories. The most striking of the pericopes, from a form-critical perspective, is the combination of the raising of the ruler's daughter and the healing of the woman with an issue of blood. The two stories are substantially complete in themselves and this combination (with the parallels) is unique among the Synoptic miracle stories. The controversy and miracle stories are readily identified and are probably traditional items. How has Matthew brought them together?

THE LINEAR ANALYSIS

The first step in the search for Matthew's plan in 9:10–34 is a study of the placing of the Hosea text and the meaning which Matthew assigns to it. It occurs in the midst of the reply of Jesus to the Pharisees' question to the disciples, "Why does your master eat with tax collectors and sinners?" The citation may break a parallelism in the reply, for without the text, the answer would read:

> Those who are well have no need of a physician, but those who are sick. For I came not to call the righteous, but sinners.

There is some reason to think that the second line, which is a theological interpretation, is a brief Christian explanation of the first.[124] If the two lines belong together, then Matthew's citation breaks the connection.

The introduction of the citation differs in form from those previously dealt with in this study. It is purely Rabbinic, a phrase often employed in

124. Bultmann, *History of the Synoptic Tradition*, 92, is probably correct in holding that the original saying contained only the Physician analogy.

Rabbinic debates.[125] "Go and learn what this means." The text, as cited, "I desire mercy and not sacrifice," is the same as that found in LXX^A and is a direct translation of the Hebrew. Thus it provides us with no evidence about the source of the quotation.

The major question that must be asked of Matthew is, "Why is the text placed here? How does it relate to this context?" Fortunately Matthew has employed the text in a second and parallel passage so that the evidence of the two uses may be drawn together to answer these questions. In 12:7 the Hosea text is an insertion into the controversy about eating grain on the Sabbath:

> And if you had known what this means, "I desire mercy and not sacrifice," you would not have condemned the guiltless.

The parallels to the application of Hos 6:6 in 9:13 are striking.

> Go and learn what this means . . .
>
> If you had known what this means . . .

In both cases the opponents are the Pharisees. The repetition of the text in 12:7 is introduced so as to say, "You didn't learn your lesson, did you?" Moreover, after both citations an application is given in the form of a *for* clause (Gk. *γάρ*):

> "For I came not to call the righteous, but sinners" (9:13).
>
> "For the Son of Man is lord of the sabbath" (12:8).

So much formal similarity probably requires that the application of the text be understood by Matthew in the same way in the two instances. And the similarity of the two lines which apply the text to the specific setting by *for* renders the judgment difficult as to whether it is the text which is interpolated or both text and application.[126]

In 9:10–13 the problem is that of table fellowship with non-kosher persons, tax-collectors and sinners. In 12:1–8 the problem is that of breaking a Sabbath regulation because of hunger. Because he cites the Hosea text as applicable to both, Matthew shows that he understands the guiding principle in such problems of Torah piety[127] to be placing of mercy above sacrifice.

125. See Stendahl, *School,* 129. The form is *πορευθέντες δὲ μάθετε τί ἐστιν* plural for צא ולמד. Also, Strack-Billerbeck, *Kommentar,* I, 499.

126. Thus, the Marcan parallel of the first passage, Mk 2:15–17, without the cited text, has strong claim to priority if the text is a Matthean insertion. In the second instance, however, Mark gives as a reason for the conclusion, "so the Son of Man is lord even of the sabbath," the general saying, "The sabbath was made for man and not man for the sabbath," which is not as congruent with the context as Mt's use of the Hosea text. The parallels thus point in both directions and do not solve the question of the origin of the Hosea texts and the applications.

127. While the rules of table fellowship derive from oral Torah (cf. Strack-Billerbeck, I, 498–499), the question of work on the Sabbath stemmed from firm Pentateuchal commandment, Ex 35:1f., for example.

Thus he interprets *sacrifice* not as cultic ritual but as literalistic observance of the *minor* rules of the oral and written Torah. Through Hos 6:6 Matthew establishes the principle that where Torah-piety and the interests of mercy conflict, mercy should prevail.

Is there any relationship between the material in Mt 9:14–34 and the principle enunciated in the use of the Hos 6:6 citation in vs. 13? Perhaps there is. Each of the following pericopes brings to the fore a problem of Torah-piety in relation to mercy and Jesus' response to the problem.

In vss. 14–17, the problem raised is that of fasting. There is only one fast required in the Pentateuch, on the Day of Atonement (Lev 16:29), but, as the question implies, there were other fasts observed, especially by the Pharisees, who fasted twice a week.[128] The original pericope may have been concerned solely with the disciples of John (with Pharisees a Matthean or early church addition). In that case the question may have meant, "Why do the disciples of Jesus, and Jesus himself, not mourn for John?"[129] The impact of that specific problem having been long since lost, the church (or Matthew) altered the passage to a question about fasts in general. Jesus rejects fasting because of the fact of his presence with the disciples (vss. 15–17). Probably this explains, for Matthew, why the church now does fast (cf. 6:16) although it knows the tradition that Jesus did not. At any rate, fasting as enjoined by Torah piety is not in order because the disciples should rejoice over Jesus' presence. Mercy (allowing the disciples to rejoice) takes precedence over sacrifice (fasting).

The next pericope, 18–26, is a doubled pericope concerning two miracles performed by Jesus, the raising of the ruler's daughter and the healing of the woman's hemorrhage. There is good reason to think that Matthew relates them both to questions of Torah piety. In the case of the ruler's daughter, Matthew is careful to say that the daughter has already died (ἄρτι ἐτελεύτησεν vs. 18). This meant that Jesus was asked to go and touch a corpse, for the ruler is explicit: "but come and lay your hand on her, and she will live." The uncleanness engendered by a corpse was serious. Touching a corpse rendered a man unclean for seven days and he was then clean only if he performed certain lustrations (Num 19:11–13). Therefore there were elaborate precautions against contracting such uncleanness (*Mishnah, Oholoth* 8:1ff.) and for identifying such uncleanness. Wherever possible such uncleanness was to be avoided. In Jesus' unhesitating willingness to go and touch the girl, Matthew offers a further specific instance of the principle of mercy over sacrifice.

128. Strack-Billerbeck, II, on Lk 18:12.

129. See the discussion in Taylor, *Mark*, 208–210. I have pressed the possibility further because the question is not as general as most controversy questions are. It seems to require a certain fast, and one of mourning over John the Baptist fits not only the question but Jesus' answer.

The miracle story that is sandwiched into the story of the ruler's daughter is also a story concerned with the healing of someone who was ritually unclean. In normal circumstances, a woman was judged unclean for seven days after the beginning of her menstrual flow. But when a discharge persisted, the uncleanness also persisted and the person was unclean until the flow stopped and seven days had passed (Lev 15:25–30). A person who touched such an unclean woman was unclean until sundown of that day and then clean only if proper washing was done. The unclean woman also conveys uncleanness by her touch (see *Mishnah, Zabim* 5:1). The situation in Mt 9:20–22 is specific. The woman is unclean and, hoping to be healed, touches Jesus' garment; thereby the garment and Jesus are rendered unclean at least until evening. Under strict observance of Torah piety the woman would have done Jesus a great disfavor, and he would have been forced to retire from normal contacts until the next day. Jesus is not angered by the woman's impertinence but commends her for her faith and grants her desire for healing. Again, mercy has taken precedence over Torah piety/sacrifice.

The next story concerns the healing of two blind men. The theme of mercy is injected into the story by the victims in their plea for help, "Have mercy on us, Son of David" (vs. 27c). The situation of the blind in ancient times has been little realized or commented upon. The blind, like cripples and lepers, were not allowed within cities but had to eke out a wretched existence outside the walls.[130] They had no legal rights whatsoever, being unable to claim possession even of items they might find. In the Talmud the blind, the leper, the childless, and the pauper are compared to the dead (*Ned.* 64b), probably because they can leave no inheritance. As a consequence of this attitude, the blind lived as beggars outside the cities. Thus, "and as Jesus passed on from there," means that as he left the city he encountered the blind men. There was no way they could live under such conditions and not be unclean. Their plea for mercy is genuine. Jesus must risk contact with uncleanness to touch them. That is what Jesus does. "Then he touched their eyes, saying, 'According to your faith be it done to you'" (vs. 29). Again, mercy takes precedence over the claims of Torah piety.

The last miracle in the series is the healing by exorcism of a dumb demoniac. What was said earlier in the treatment of the Beelzebul controversy applies fully to this passage. In order to heal the man, Jesus must risk the criticism from his opponents that he acts in concert with the demons, that he is a magician who knows how to achieve real contact with them. The response of the Pharisees is the charge of collusion with Beelzebul just as in ch. 12. Again, Jesus risks an act which goes beyond careful piety in order to

130. *The Jewish Encyclopedia*, ed. by I. Singer, III, the article on "The blind in law and literature," 248–249.

be merciful. In Matthew's view, the explanation for these unorthodox actions on the part of Jesus and the disciples is the claim of mercy over sacrifice.

THE ANALYSIS AND THE CONTROLS

The number of Matthean characteristics in support of the linear analysis of 9:10–34 is not as extensive as in the previous passages analyzed. However, there are indications of the author's work. They are:

1) The mention of the Pharisees in vs. 14 and their hostile comment in vs. 34 appear to be extraneous to the material in which they occur but important to Matthew.
2) The similarity in form of the citation of Hos 6:6 in 9:13 and 12:7 provides an important clue to Matthew's understanding of the text. The introductory formula is similar. The application made to Torah piety is similar. And the *for* (γάρ) introductions to the following clauses are parallel.
3) The defense of non-kosher eating habits, which was the theme of 15:1–20, is the theme of 9:10–13 and is of apparent concern for Matthew.

In spite of these characteristics, it must be said that the author has not heavily altered the traditions he has taken up by words and phrases, or interpretive comments, that are peculiarly his own. The major thrust of the analysis must, therefore, be supported from the other controls.

The second control, logical pattern, is at first sight not significantly more applicable than the first. No readily discernible logical pattern combines these traditions into a unified whole. However, when the technique which Matthew employed to comment upon Isa 42:1–4 in 12:22–50 is recalled, the case is altered. There, passages were related directly to the OT text rather than to one another in consecutive order. In the light of first-century Jewish (and specifically Pharisaic) rules about eating and about defilement, a central theme does emerge from the collection of stories. Problems about table fellowship and fasting clearly related to the Christian conflict with Jews over Torah piety. Further, when it is observed that the raising of the ruler's daughter (laying one's hand on a corpse), the healing of the woman with a hemorrhage (a *zab,* or unclean person), the touching of two blind beggars (who lived in uncleanness outside the city), and the healing of a demoniac (thus risking contact with the world of demons), are all activities which bring Jesus into tension with the requirements of Torah piety and are situations which should be avoided, then a logical pattern does appear to have brought the various traditions together.

It is clear that Matthew treats such conflicts of interest under the general rule which he sees stated in the Hosea text; namely, that the demands of mercy supersede those of Torah piety (understood as sacrifice). The control of logical pattern combined with the relationship to the OT text supports the general thrust of the analysis.

Because this analysis has not revealed as tightly knit an organization around the OT text, because the fasting question is slightly at odds with the themes of the rest of the chapter and because there is no call to exegetical assent, this analysis is not as compelling as any of the three previous analyses. Nevertheless, the theme of mercy has been demonstrated clearly enough in the passage to provide strong reason to believe that Matthew shaped the section around his understanding of Hos 6:6.

THE ANALYSIS AND FORM CRITICISM

There are three instances in which the analysis of 9:10–34 has an effect on form critical concerns. First, it was observed that the citation of Hos 6:6 in 9:13 was an insertion into the table-fellowship controversy. It was further observed that in 12:7 the same text was cited *followed* in vs. 8 by a clause formally similar to that in 9:13. The direct and theological character of the application, "for I came not to call the righteous, but sinners," of the physician analogy, and the formal similarity to Matthean pericopes involving the *same* type of insertion and the same text, may suggest that Matthew is responsible for all of vs. 13. In both 9:13 and 12:8 the *for* clause may be a Matthean interpretive addition based on his understanding of Hos 6:6.

Secondly, the uniqueness of the question of fasting in the section was revealed by the analysis. The reason given for fasting is only remotely one of mercy (it may be understood as, "Be merciful and let the disciples enjoy his company before he is gone"). The formal similarity between the questions about fasting and table fellowship becomes important. Both are initiated by questions about the disciples' activity. The replies to both questions are enigmatic parables. It is natural to suppose that they belonged together in the tradition and that Matthew has followed the tradition (written or oral) without making any major attempt to adjust the fasting question to his understanding of Hos 6:6.

The third instance significant for form criticism occurs in the double miracle of 9:18–26. The linear analysis has revealed a reason for the conjunction of the two miracles. Both deal with matters of obvious and serious defilement according to Jewish law. Both types of defilement are dealt with in the Pentateuch and are not just matters of oral tradition. The combination of the two, as it occurs in Matthew, requires a perception of the defilement questions on the part of the one who made the combination. While this does not mean it was Matthew, it does mean that the combination is likely to have been made in a Jewish-Christian environment. The fact that the longer accounts of both parts of the story in Mark and Luke do not take up this defilement theme but develop along other lines suggests that in

Matthew's form the rationale for the original combination (defilement questions) remains clear whether by Matthew's revision of the Mk-Lk form, or his use of a Jewish-Christian source, or by his own combination of the stories.

THE ANALYSIS AND THE SYNOPTIC PROBLEM

In favor of the view that Matthew used Mark for this section is the fact that virtually all of the material in the section is paralleled in Mark. Moreover, the insertion of Hos 6:6 in Mt 9:13 and 12:7 occurs in passages with Marcan parallels but in which the text is lacking. It can hardly be contested that Matthew has used some sources for the composition of this section of the gospel. The demonstration of the theme of compassion would help to explain the combination of two controversy stories from the early Marcan collection (2:1-3:6) with the double miracle found in Mk 5:21–43. Of the analyses thus far, this one does no damage to the two-document hypothesis, but supports it. The only outstanding problems stem from the *for* clauses in Mt 9:13 and 12:8 and from Mark's much more dramatic narration of the double miracle which may suggest possible novelistic adaptation by Mark. However, these problems are not overwhelming and it is possible, though not strictly necessary, to suppose that Mt 9:10–34 has been constructed by Matthew from Mark.

THE ANALYSIS AND MATTHEAN REDACTION

The linear analysis of Mt 9:10–34 has further confirmed a number of the suggestions about Matthew's techniques and purposes which had been gained in the first three analyses. A special application of Hos 6:6 to the problems of Christian attitudes toward Torah piety is another example of his method of interpreting the OT. The emphasis on controversy with the Pharisees, and on conflicts which thoroughly fit the historical situation of Jewish Christianity as we can perceive it from other material, confirms the view of Matthew gained in the discussion of the Beelzebul controversy and the clean-unclean debate.

A major step forward is also possible as a result of this analysis. Matthew's use of Hos 6:6 provides a reader with a glimpse of the way in which Matthew, and perhaps the Jewish-Christian church of which he was a part, reasoned in instances where the demands of their understanding of the gospel contravened the oral or written Torah. Extrapolating from the tradition about Jesus what appeared to him to be the guiding principle in such cases, Matthew derived the principle of "mercy over sacrifice." The Torah was not to be taken lightly and breaches of Torah piety should always be done only for the sake of compassion. This principle allowed table fellowship with Gentiles and sinners. It allowed the healing and helping of the ritually unclean. Compassion was a part of the Jesus tradition and a guiding principle of Christian life. An incorporation of this exegetically based evidence about Matthew's understanding of the law into a treatment such as that by G. Barth on Matthew's interpretation of the law is essential.[131]

ANALYSIS 5: MT 11:7–15 AND MAL 3:1

Another text which exhibits signs of the Matthean mid-point technique is the citation of Mal 3:1 in 11:10. In the passage Jesus comments on the crowds about John the Baptist (vs. 7). Jesus asks, "What did you come out to see when you went to the desert to see John?" (vss. 7–9). After the question a number of possible, but inadequate, answers are given. The correct answer is then given by citation of Mal 3:1:

> This is he of whom it is written, "Behold I send my messenger before thy face, who shall prepare thy way before thee" (11:10).

After the citation, Jesus continues by stressing the greatness and yet comparative insignificance of John (vss. 11–13). He closes with a direct statement that John was the forerunner *Elijah*. The last phrase in the passage (vs. 15) is the call to assent, "He who has ears to hear, let him hear."

The pericope has no readily identifiable formal structure. It may be an interpretive comment shaped for this context. The Malachi citation is necessary for the logical structure because it provides the referent for the forerunner idea (vs. 14). At what stage in the tradition the passage took shape cannot be determined from the form alone. Within the pericope, however, there is a logion of some importance, Mt 11:11–12. Vs. 12, especially, is not only difficult to interpret but is also difficult to apply to the context. An authentic logion from Jesus concerning John probably has been incorporated into the passage because of its topical relation to the subject matter.

131. Barth's treatment of 9:13 and 12:7 (*Tradition and Interpretation in Matthew*, 82–83) is weak for two reasons. 1) Barth limits the principle of mercy versus sacrifice so much that it does not deal with instances of breaking the ceremonial law. The reason for this limitation is his correct grasp of Mt's respect for the law elsewhere. The very fact that the latter is true is the reason for Matthew's formulating a rationale for Christian exceptions. 2) Barth does not recognize the importance of mercy and compassion in the material following 9:13 and the number of specific regulations that are there superseded by Jesus' mercy. Mt is, in many ways, a stern and forbidding taskmaster (cf. the antitheses in ch. 5, the rebuke to the Pharisees in ch. 23, the rigor of the disciples' mission in ch. 10, and the rules of conduct in ch. 18). Therefore, his formulation of this principle of mercy is very important to his understanding of Jesus and of the Christian life.

A LINEAR ANALYSIS OF MT 11:7–15

Jesus' reply (11:4–6) to the question of the messengers from John has provided the setting for a discussion about John. That reply alluded to a Messianic text from Isaiah, Isa 35:1–10. The following pericope brings to the forefront not only the subject of John the Baptist but also the question of the relationship between John and Jesus as it has been posed by the exchange of question and answer in 11:2–6. Therefore, an interpretive comment to the crowd about John is thoroughly appropriate to the context.[132]

There is nothing in vss. 7–9 which would indicate Matthean authorship or even his editorial work. The series of questions and possible solutions appears to be traditional. The introduction to the citation, however, may be the work of Matthew. In Mt 3:3, speaking of John the Baptist, Matthew introduces Isa 40:3 in the following way:

"For this is he who was spoken of by the prophet Isaiah when he said. . . ."

Now in 11:10 another comment about John is introduced in similar fashion:

"This is he of whom it is written. . . ."

These are the only instances in the Synoptic tradition (Mt 11:10/Lk 7:27) where a citation is directly applied to a person in this fashion. Both texts identify John the Baptist as the fulfillment of the Malachi text. One or the other or both of the citation formulas, therefore, might reflect the work of Matthew.[133] The text itself, is again too brief to allow definitive comment on its form. Matthew (as well as Mk and Lk) has *κατασκευάσει* for *prepare* as compared to the LXX *ἐπιβλέψεται*. This change appears to be essential to the meaning of the text for Christians, however, and it need not, and probably does not, stem from Matthew's work.

The material following the citation is a further comment on the meaning of John the Baptist:

> Truly I say to you, among those born of women there has risen no one greater than John the Baptist; yet he who is least in the kingdom of heaven is greater than he. From the days of John the Baptist until now the kingdom of heaven has suffered violence, and men of violence take it by force. For all the prophets and the law prophesied until John; and if you are willing to accept it, he is Elijah who is to come. He who has ears to hear, let him hear (11:11–15).

There are strong indications that Matthew has shaped the first comparison. The phrase, "he who is least in the kingdom of heaven," reflects a common way of designating the disciples in Matthew (25:40,45 with *ἐλάχιστος*, with *μικρός* in 10:42; 18:6,10, and 14). The problem of com-

132. On the natural connection of the passages, see Creed, *St. Luke*, 104–105.

133. Stendahl (*School*, 50) briefly notes the parallel between the two formulas but he does not gather the positive and negative evidence which strengthens the connection.

parison in the kingdom of heaven is also familiar from Mt 5:19. Moreover, the use of μικρότερος instead of ἐλάχιστος in the phrase for the disciples may show an awareness of the earlier comparison (Mt 5:19, "Whoever then relaxes one of the least [τῶν ἐλαχίστων] of these commandments and teaches men so, shall be called least [ἐλάχιστος] in the kingdom of heaven"). While it may be asking too much of Matthew to realize that "least in the kingdom of heaven" was a negative phrase in 5:19, it is still true that he has avoided any inconsistency in his use of *little* and *least.*

Though "among those born of women" is a stock Jewish phrase and might have been taken over from a source (only here in the Synoptics, but cf. 1 Cor 11:12 and Gal 4:4), it does fit well in a Jewish-Christian milieu.

The meaning of the comparison of John to the least in the kingdom must be taken quite seriously. Of all men, John the Baptist was greatest, but even he is placed below those who are a part of the kingdom of heaven. The disciples will have first place in the kingdom, and even the least will be more important than the great John. Especially in view of the fact that this passage comes so soon after the discourse on discipleship in ch. 10, this meaning must be Matthew's.[134]

The next verse is very problematical. It is difficult to interpret in either its Matthean or Lucan context. As a result of this obscurity, many scholars have assigned the saying to Jesus himself.[135]

> From the days of John the Baptist until now the kingdom of heaven has suffered violence, and men of violence take it by force (11:12).

Yet, even when the grammatical and interpretive difficulty is noted,[136] there is an indication that the argument for authenticity may be wrong. "From the days of John the Baptist until now" (in Lk 16:16 without *until now*) implies a clear time interval. If the words were spoken by Jesus, they had to cover such an extremely narrow limit of time that the saying would probably have been unclear to the hearers. However, if the logion speaks of the experience of the later church put into the mouth of Jesus, the natural reference is to the struggles of the zealots and the Romans over Palestine which culminated in the war of 66–70 A.D. The reluctance on the part of scholars to allow so geographical a sense to the kingdom of heaven has already been challenged by the evidence for an earthly Matthean conception

134. McNeile's attempt to moderate the saying by speaking of a present condition of John vs. a future one for the kingdom is not convincing (*Matthew,* 154). The kingdom is future for Mt, but the divisions there relate to the present. Mt should be taken to mean what he says, even if he is less than generous to non-disciples.

135. Authenticity is strongly urged by C. H. Dodd, *The Parables of the Kingdom,* (rev. ed.; New York: Charles Scribner's Sons, 1961), 32–33, but doubted by Bultmann, *The History,* 164–165.

136. The primary difficulty lies with the meaning of βιάζεται in Lk or ἁρπάζουσιν in Mt. The words require, in any case, some picture of an assault on the kingdom.

of the kingdom in ch. 13.[137] Nor is there any hint whatsoever in the saying itself, apart from its context, which would allow an interpretation that it deals with the Pharisees and Herod in their opposition to John. The Romans and the Zealots were men of violence. It can scarcely be shown that Pharisees or tax-collectors were so regarded by anyone in the early church.[138]

The next verse in the passage (11:13) is crucial for Matthew:

> For all the prophets and the law prophesied until John.

The implication is that with John some change was made. In ch. 12 and in ch. 13 Matthew looks to the OT as a whole for prophecies concerning the Messiah. They prophesied. But John was more than a prophet, vs. 9, John did not just prophesy. John prepared the way.

> And if you are willing to accept it, he is Elijah who is to come. He who has ears to hear, let him hear (11:14–15).

Because John was the forerunner Elijah, because he was the messenger sent before Jesus, he was greater than a prophet and he brought the line of Messianic prophecy to an end. He was the forerunner of the Messiah. With the call to exegetical assent in vs. 15, Matthew signifies his belief that vss. 11–14 are a demonstration of the application of vs. 10 to John the Baptist.

THE ANALYSIS AND THE CONTROLS

Even though this is a very short passage in Matthew, there are several points at which the analysis is supported by the redactional controls. The conjunction of the two styles of introductory phrase, 3:3 and 11:10, in two passages about the same person and the same OT text suggests that the connection is Matthew's. Vs. 11 reflects not only Jewish but also Matthean idiom in the phrase "the least in the kingdom of heaven." The saying in vs. 12 can be understood as Matthew's view of the hostilities between Jewish patriots and the Romans which resulted in the Jewish War. The call for exegetical assent is used in conjunction with a comment following an OT text, just as in 13:9,43, and 15:10.

The logical structure of the passage is evident only in the light of the Malachi citation. The key line of the passage is vs. 14, where the role of John the Baptist is made explicit. "And if you are willing to accept it, he [John] is Elijah who is to come." That statement is a direct application of Mal 3:1 to

137. Conzelmann is justified in this position for Lk (*Theology*, 115) but Lk's view of the kingdom is not Mt's.

138. After conceding that the Mt-Lk contexts afforded the saying are irrelevant and that Mt's form of the saying is probably older, W. Wink goes on to argue for a connection to the Pharisees. That depends on Lk's context: Walter Wink, *John the Baptist in the Gospel Tradition* (Cambridge: Cambridge University Press, 1968), 20–22.

John the Baptist. It is based on the Jewish expectation of Elijah as a precursor.[139] The explanation is careful, however, not to allow too high an estimate of John as precursor. For, even though he was a great figure, yet he stood outside the community which would inherit the highest place in the kingdom of heaven (vs. 11). All of this is logical and is thus another instance of Matthew's mid-point use of an OT text.

THE ANALYSIS AND MATTHEAN REDACTION

In addition to further confirmation of the hypothesis that Matthew shapes portions of the gospel by using the OT, this analysis further strengthens the view that the gospel is written by a Jewish-Christian in a Jewish-Christian milieu. He has taken up the Elijah expectation in Judaism and supported it with the appropriate OT citation. He makes a direct and dogmatic assertion that John the Baptist was Elijah, and then he attempts to show the subordination of this John/Elijah to Jesus and the church. There is no element in the passage which runs counter to the view of Matthew already gained in the preceding analyses. The addition of the John/Elijah parallel serves only to strengthen and amplify the picture of the work of Matthew as a Jewish-Christian author conversant with Jewish traditions and clever in making them serve his Christian purposes.

ANALYSIS 6: MT 10:34–39 AND MIC 7:6

A final instance of the use of an OT text as the logical center of a passage occurs in 10:34–39. There, in a passage which discusses the divisions among men which Jesus' call to discipleship inevitably causes, an allusion is made (10:34–36) to Mic 7:6.

> Do not think that I have come to bring peace on earth; I have not come to bring peace, but a sword. For I have come to set a man against his father, and a daughter against her mother, and a daughter-in-law against her mother-in-law; and a man's foes will be those of his own household.
>
> For the son treats the father with contempt, the daughter rises up against her mother, the daughter-in-law against her mother-in-law; a man's enemies are the men of his own house (Mic 7:6).

The allusion is followed in 10:37–39 by:

> He who loves father or mother more than me is not worthy of me; and he who loves son or daughter more than me is not worthy of me; and he who does not take his cross and follow me is not worthy of me. He who finds his life will lose it, and he who loses his life for my sake will find it.

139. J. Jeremias, *TDNT*, II, "Ἠλ(ε)ίας." 930-943.

The passage, with its primary message that of the cost of discipleship, is set in a context which is generally reassuring to the disciples. 10:26–32 reminds the faithful that in spite of difficulty they will be favorably remembered at the judgment. 10:40–42 deals with the crucial role of the disciples for the judgment of those to whom they are sent. The overall tone of the whole discourse is one of encouragement against adversity. The disciples must face possible rejection in their mission (vs. 14) and severe persecution (vss. 16–23). The passage under consideration is a part of this argument. It serves as a reiteration of the dangers inherent in discipleship. Following the judgment sentences of 10:32–33, it fits smoothly into its immediate and its general context.

Formally, the pericope consists of three elements. The "peace vs. sword" saying is an independent logion which has been brought into this context. No item in it could be termed Matthean, and it is clear that the saying requires further explication in order for it to apply to the Matthean context of family division and discipleship. The necessary explanation is given in terms of Mic 7:6. The text is a classic expression of division among people but it is not so clearly related to "I have not come to bring peace, but a sword." The application by the conjunction *for,* (γάρ) of this text to the sword saying severely limits the meaning that may be given to *sword.*

The sentences which follow the allusion are all formally alike. Their structure is that of a conditional participle as the subject of the sentence.[140] That form appears to have drawn at least some of the sentences together since the *cross* saying in vs. 38 and the *life* saying in 39 are not closely related in theme to the *family* sayings of vs. 37.

THE LINEAR ANALYSIS

The outline of the pericope and the foregoing formal analysis provide initial insight into its construction. Apparently, the sword saying is suggested to Matthew by the preceding verses which predict division over Jesus (vss. 32–33). In turn the sword saying has been interpreted for this context by the allusive citation of Mic 7:6. Nothing in the form of that citation is significant enough to reveal the text form presupposed or any radically unique interpretation by Matthew.[141] However, the sentences which follow (vs. 37) are closely related to the text:

> He who loves father or mother more than me is not worthy of me; and he who loves son or daughter more than me is not worthy of me.

These sentences apply Mic 7:6 to the sword saying and to the question of denying and confessing Jesus, the subject of vss. 32–33, in an integrated unit.

140. On this form and the probability that such sentences are influenced by Hebrew or Aramaic see K. Beyer, *Semitische Syntax im Neuen Testament,* I (Göttingen: Vandenhoeck and Ruprecht, 1962), 210–211.

141. Stendahl, *School,* 90–91.

The requirements of discipleship will sometimes set a son against his father or a daughter against her mother. Moreover, Matthew extends the nature of the hostilities expressed in Mic 7:6 by allowing for the reverse case; that is, father and mother may also be set over against son or daughter because of allegiance to Jesus (a similar set of relationships has already been used in 10:21 in the section on persecution). The Micah text has served as a middle term for Matthew. Through it he has interpreted the sword saying as relevant to the specific context of family divisions. He has made that application perfectly clear by precise reference to the divisions within households which are spoken of in the Micah text. In this way *both* the sword saying *and* Mic 7:6 are brought to bear on the theme of the cost of discipleship.

The sentences of vss. 38 and 39 are not entirely unrelated to this context. The general context is that of proving oneself worthy of Jesus by placing allegiance to him over that to family (this is reminiscent of the discussion about family allegiances in 12:46–50). It is probably Matthew's intention to suggest that the pain of broken family relationships is a cross that some disciples must bear, "and he who does not take his cross and follow me is not worthy of me" (10:38). This is true no matter what "taking up one's cross" may have meant in other contexts. "Worthy of me" conforms the section to the preceding sentences and to the rest of the chapter, where this phrase has been prominent (vss. 11,13,37). Vs. 39 proceeds with a more general statement about the cost of discipleship. It has not been conformed to the logic of "worthy of me." Family separation and its pain are viewed by Matthew as an application of the general principle of losing one's life. It is probable that in vs. 39 Matthew has taken up a traditional saying which he believes applicable to this context and which has the necessary parallel form. Between the saying in vs. 34 and the one in vs. 39 stands an interpretation of family hostility caused by Christian faith which is built around Mic 7:6.

THE ANALYSIS AND THE CONTROLS

The steps from the sword saying in vs. 34 to Mic 7:6 and to the specific application to the Christian situation are understandable as a logical process whereby the sword saying is brought to bear on the theme of the divisions caused by allegiance to Jesus. Since the problems of family division have already appeared in the discourse (vs. 21), they are either very much a concern of the author or they are in his mind because he has just dealt with them. There is nothing in the sword saying which logically requires the citation of Mic 7:6. But neither is the citation in conflict with it. The logical theme, division caused by allegiance to Jesus, is illustrated by the use of the OT text, and then that text is carefully applied to the context. This is firm evidence of redactional work on the basis of two of the controls, the presence of an identifiable pattern and the use of the OT as a source.

The major question remaining is whether this structure is from Matthew or stems from a source used for the whole discourse. The literary relationships that were discovered come from the discipleship discourse (vs. 21//vs. 37, and the term *worthy* in vss. 11–13 and 37–38). But the problem of family tensions does come to the surface in 12:46–50, and the saying about losing one's life recurs in 16:25. This evidence in itself is inconclusive. However, coupled with the evidence from the earlier analyses that the technique of using OT passages in middle term fashion is a Matthean trait, it supports the view that 10:34–39 is Matthew's own formulation.[142]

THE ANALYSIS AND THE SYNOPTIC PROBLEM

The parallel to this passage in Lk 12:51–53 diverges greatly from the Matthean passage. The common use of a saying about peace (Lk 12:51, "Do you think that I have come to give peace on earth? No, I tell you, but rather division") suggests some literary relationship, but nothing definite can be said about the relative priority of the two passages.

THE ANALYSIS AND MATTHEW

If 10:34–38 was constructed by Matthew and reflects his concerns, then an important insight into his situation can be gained. The conflict which the application of Mic 7:6 reflects was a concern of Matthew's. It concerned him so much that he dealt with family divisions and the resultant cost of discipleship in both 10:21 and in 10:34–38. These passages, especially 10:34–38, bolster those Christians caught in such family difficulties. The historical situation which would have occasioned these difficulties was probably the process of the separation of the church from the synagogue in the late first century. Since there is firm evidence for such family pressures from the gospel of John,[143] and since the other analyses (unmistakably Matthean) have pointed to other aspects of the controversy surrounding this separation (the Beelzebul controversy, the handwashing controversy, the question of messiahship), this analysis fits very well the emerging picture of the situation in which Matthew worked. If this is true, these conflicts are not

142. 10:40–42, which follows the passage under discussion, is much more surely a composition by Mt, especially vs. 42 (see Cope, "Mt. 25:31–46, 'The Sheep and the Goats,'" 39–40). Since the same grammatical form is followed from vss. 37–42 (conditional participial phrases as subjects), there is some additional evidence that Mt has constructed the passage.

143. The analysis by J. L. Martyn of Jn 9:1–23 (*History and Theology in the Fourth Gospel,* 3–16) stresses the importance of the pressure placed on the blind man's parents by the Pharisees because of their son's acceptance of Jesus. This is an extremely likely setting for the implications of 10:34–37 in Mt.

past events for Matthew but are very much alive in the community for which he writes.[144]

A SUMMARY OF THE RESULTS OF THE SIX ANALYSES

In addition to the assessments of the individual analyses, it is valuable to draw together some of the overall results of the study of Matthew's use of the mid-point texts. In terms of their support when considered in the light of the redactional controls, I would rate the six as follows:

1) Mt 13:1–52—very strong.
   The evidence for the deliberate use of a subtle theory of parable interpretation as well as the use of two OT texts, Isa 6:9–10 and Ps 78:2 demonstrate Matthean redactional formulation.

2) Mt 12:1–50—very strong.
   Not only does the analysis provide a logic for the organization of the chapter, but it reveals a special Matthean exegesis of Isa 42:1–4. The logical structure of the Beelzebul controversy, based on the Matthean understanding of Isa 42:1–4, is strong evidence of redaction by Matthew.

3) Mt 15:1–20—very strong.
   The logic which Matthew employs in explaining how Isa 29:13 relates to the handwashing question is in exact accord with the Jewish-Christian nature of the material.

4) Mt 9:10–34—probable.
   Unquestionably this analysis depends on the success of the first three analyses for some of its support. Even so, there are distinct evidences of Matthean characteristics. The "mercy and not sacrifice" contrast of Hos 6:6 dominates the section as Matthew has constructed it.

5) Mt 11:7–15—strong.
   The evidence that Matthew has structured the passage around Mal 3:1 is very strong for so short a passage. Vss. 14 and 15, clearly Matthean, can only be understood as a direct application of the Mal 3:1 text to John the Baptist.

6) Mt 10:34–39—probable.
   The logical connections between the Mic 7:6 text and the material immediately before and after it are the most important evidence of Matthew's mid-point technique in this passage. The analysis results in

144. For the view that Mt is using an older source see D. R. A. Hare, *The Theme of Jewish Persecution,* 96f. But the literary evidence favors a view that the passage reflects Mt's work. For if Mt is using a source, the parallel in Lk suggests that the source is Q, and unless Q was like Mt here and, therefore, stems from the time of separation of church and synagogue (a difficult position for anyone to hold) then the precision of the application in 10:34–38 is Mt's own.

a picture of Matthew's situation that is thoroughly in line with that of analyses 2 and 3.

One may debate the relative strength of one or two of the individual analyses without destroying the general result. That result is a critically defensible linear analysis of about 150 verses of Matthew's text. In all of these analyses the skillful work of the evangelist in employing the OT to suit his own purposes has been the primary key to his way of writing and thinking. In six of the seven cases of OT citation and exegesis, the evangelist developed a very subtle and unique set of connections between the text and the gospel context. The net result of the six analyses is powerful support for the working hypothesis that Matthew was a Jewish-Christian author thoroughly familiar with the OT and with Jewish traditions of its interpretation and that he used this knowledge as a key to his organization of several portions of his gospel.

In addition to the cumulative strength of this evidence about the use of the OT, the analyses also reveal a tendency of Matthew to reuse and interweave subjects and favorite themes. The Beelzebul charge is treated in chs. 9, 10, and 12; the importance of the spoken word at the judgment is used in the Beelzebul controversy (12:22–37) and in the clean-unclean debate (5:1–20); the tree and its fruit imagery recurs in chs. 7, 12, and 15; the call to exegetical understanding is found in 13:9 and 43 and 11:15, and in modified form in 13:13 and 23 and in 15:10. These interconnections of theme and motif occur not just in midpoint contexts but in other parts of the gospel. For example, the image of the blind guides occurs in a mid-point passage (15:14) and in the discourse against the Pharisees (23:16), but it is related to the same subject matter, binding vows. These interwoven themes suggest the work of an author who is shaping the tradition to suit his purposes.

This leads to a further result. A pattern of motif and subject matter has emerged which is closely related to the problems of Jewish Christianity in its struggle with Pharisaic Judaism. Matthew brings the Pharisees into the limelight of every struggle. The Beelzebul debate is shaped around a Messianic claim which refutes a Pharisaic charge that may have been leveled against Matthew and his church. The problems of ritual handwashing and of table fellowship with sinners and tax-collectors also reflect an historical conflict between the two religious parties. The analysis of 10:34–38 suggests that families are being divided by the conflict. Not only do all of these items, when linked together, suggest the historical situation in which the gospel was written, but none of the material thus far examined militates against such a setting. This evidence, coinciding as it does with the evidence of Matthew's skilled use of the OT, is very important for determing the historical situation of Matthew and his church.

Finally, it should be noted that the evidence has suggested, in diverse ways, that Matthew must be taken as a Jewish-Christian author. The

Qumran-like understanding of the interpretation of the parables in ch. 13, the exact knowledge of defilement questions in ch. 8, and the precision of the answer in the clean-unclean debate can lead in no other direction. Moreover, this cannot be a trait assigned to one of Matthew's sources. The passages involved in the analyses are from too wide a range of the gospel. The same Jewish-Christian features emerge in discourse (ch. 13), in controversies (12:22–37 and 15:1–20) and in miracle narratives (9:18–26). Exponents of other views about Matthew must come to terms with this strong evidence for a Jewish-Christian author.

The analyses are also important for questions of source criticism. The evidence for Matthean structure and thought in these passages must now be considered as evidence in the discussion of Synoptic relationships. In 12:22–37, 13:1–52, and 15:1–20, some of the evidence of Matthean structure indicates a need for further research into the relationship of redactional structure to source analysis.

Form critically the analyses have held few surprises. Some passages have been shown to belong to Matthew's work rather than to tradition. This would have been expected in any successful linear analysis. The most important general form-critical insight involves the structure of the controversy story. Scholars have long recognized the question-counterquestion form and its importance in the gospels; the analysis of the Beelzebul and the clean-unclean debates suggests that this was the form of those passages in the original tradition.

Finally, these six analyses have shown that the proposed method of redaction criticism is applicable to Matthew, that Matthew has employed some of the OT texts in his gospel in such a way that they provide the logical transition and organizational principles for the passages in which they occur (mid-point texts). The analyses have also produced some firm evidence that Matthew wrote as a Jewish-Christian for a Christian community which was in sharp conflict with Pharisaic Judaism.

CHAPTER 3

THE FUNCTION OF OTHER OLD TESTAMENT TEXTS IN MATTHEW

The six analyses of the preceding chapter have established that Matthew employed a number of OT texts as pivotal elements in the construction of his gospel. That technique was called mid-point construction. In each case the OT text was the logical center for the linear reading of the passage. Clearly, this is one way that a source, the OT, has been used by Matthew in writing the gospel.

There are a number of other ways in which a source may be used by a writer. The source may be incorporated into a passage in which it simply serves as one stepping stone in an argument. Or the source may be cited simply as a relevant example with no further use made of it. Between the extreme of simple citation as example and the formation of a passage around the source material, as in the mid-point examples, there lies a considerable range of possibilities for the use of a source. Therefore, it is appropriate to ask at this point in this study whether other ways in which Matthew has employed the OT texts can be detected and what these may reveal about his work.

There are quite a number of references to OT passages in Matthew, either by citation or allusion, which simply serve as stepping stones in the construction of the pericopes in which they occur, integral parts in the flow of thought. The best examples are found in the antitheses in Mt 5 and in the controversies which involve OT texts.[1] In such cases, the use of the OT provides no useful clue to the work of Matthew.

There are, in addition to these texts, three fulfillment citations which are simple and direct citations that have not influenced the passages which precede or follow them. In Mt 4:15–16, Isa 9:1–2 is cited as a prophetic validation of the place where Jesus began his ministry. Matthew has probably added the names of Zebulun and Naphtali to the mention of Capernaum in vs. 13, but the addition is geographically accurate and tells us only that Matthew knew something about the ancient geography of Palestine. In a similar way, Isa 40:3 is cited in Mt 3:3. Throughout the baptism narrative and throughout the gospel (11:10–14 and 17:11–12) Matthew treats John the Baptist as the prophesied forerunner of the Messiah, but there are no literary or logical reasons for claiming that Isa 40:3 has influenced the

1. OT texts appear in 5:21,27,31,33, and 38 in the antitheses, and in the context of controversies in 15:4; 19:4–5 and 18; 22:24,32,37,39, and 44. Other instances of texts which occur in simple connection with their contexts may be seen in 9:36; 21:13,16; 23:39; 26:31,64.

construction of the surrounding material. Isa 53:4 is cited in Mt 8:17 as a fulfillment of the healings of Jesus which were summarized in vs. 16. Again, there is no apparent relationship between the citation and the wording of the preceding summary and no relationship between the text and the pericopes which follow. In these instances, Matthew has not used the OT in a way which tells us any more about him than that he is fond of using fulfillment texts.

There is at least one instance in Matthew where an OT text is treated in almost direct reversal of the mid-point technique. The citation of Ps 118:22–23 at the conclusion of the parable of the Wicked Tenants, Mt 21:42, stands within an interpretive section and is largely ignored. It is clear in all three gospels that the reason for citing this text is the killing of the son by the tenants (Mt 21:38–39). This son is "The stone which the builders rejected . . ." (Ps 118:22). However, only Luke makes any further connection of this popular Christian proof text[2] with the surrounding passage. In view of the evidence that Matthew often weaves the text and subsequent context together, the lack of connection is surprising and must mean that the text stood in Matthew's source and does not originate with him.[3] This does not mean that Matthew disagrees with the citation and its purpose. He probably does agree that the casting out and killing of the son was rejecting the cornerstone. But the interpretive verses in 21:41,43,45 are not triggered by the text.

What is it that has prompted the interpretation? The verses read:

41 They said to him, "He will put those wretches to a miserable death, and let out the vineyard to other tenants who will give him the fruits in their seasons."

43 Therefore I tell you, the kingdom of God will be taken away from you and given to a nation producing the fruits of it.

45 When the chief priests and the Pharisees heard his parables, they perceived that he was speaking about them.

Evidence that Matthew has been at work in these verses is abundant. Vss. 41 and 45 are substantially triple tradition but vs. 43 is found only in Matthew. More important, the elements of vss. 41 and 43 are organized in precise parallelism, including the Matthean phrase about "the fruits." The vineyard is the kingdom of God. The tenants are "you," and vs. 45 makes it clear that "you" are the chief priests and the Pharisees. The other tenants are "a nation producing the fruits of the kingdom of God."

This passage has often been viewed as a reflection of the turning of the Christian mission from the Jews to the Gentiles.[4] The support for this is the

2. A discussion of the use of Ps 118 in the NT is given by B. Lindars, *New Testament Apologetic*, 169–174.

3. This would support the priority of Mk but would not preclude the existence of this parable with this proof text attached in the preliterary tradition.

4. Cf. Strecker, *Der Weg*, 33,110–113.

clear contrast between the wicked tenants who once were stewards of the kingdom and the new nation (ἔθνος), presumably no longer Judaism. If this line of interpretation is correct, then the passage stands in sharp contradiction to the evidence for Matthew's Jewish orientation which was gathered in the analysis of the *mid-point* passages.

There are good critical reasons for questioning the Jew vs. Gentile interpretation of these verses, however. Nation (ἔθνος) should not be equated with the nations or Gentiles (ἔθνη) as such interpretation requires. The singular term occurs only twice in Matthew, here and in the apocalyptic formula in 24:7, "nation will rise against nation." That traditional verse can be of no help in interpreting this one. So the meaning here must come from the context.

Moreover, the passage does not allow the reader to think of Gentiles or of one Gentile nation. When the tenants were punished in the destruction of 70 A.D., the ones who took over Palestine were the Romans. No one will contend that *nation* here means Romans and that this passage is a pro-Roman one.

Finally, the contrast is clearly that of wicked tenants who do not give fruit to the owner and new tenants who will give the fruits. The *nation* which will bear the fruits is almost certainly the Christian community. This is confirmed by the uses of the concept of yielding fruits elsewhere in the gospel of Matthew (3:8,10; 7:17–19; 12:33) which are clearly related to the Christian life. That correlation is explicit in the interpretation of the parable of the Sower where the one who hears the word of the kingdom of God and understands it "bears fruit."[5]

Therefore, Mt 21:41–45 does not run counter to the evidence from the *mid-point* analysis that Matthew is a Jewish-Christian author; on the contrary, it supports it. As Tagawa says,

> It is clear that Matthew is thinking (in vs. 43) of the Church which is in the process of formation. The fact that the Christian community is here called ἔθνος corresponds to the usage of λαός in 1:21 where the Church is understood as the true Israel. The evangelist here criticizes Pharisaic Judaism from the standpoint of the Christian Church. So this text has nothing to do with the Gentile-Jewish antithesis.[6]

What is gained positively from this passage for our purpose is, however, significant. It is possible for Matthew to ignore an OT citation when it does not serve his interpretive purposes.

There are also some passages in Matthew which do exhibit evidence of shaping with reference to the OT texts but which cannot properly be termed *mid-point* texts. A clear example of this is the citation of Zech 9:9 in Mt

5. W. Trilling presents a similar analysis showing that the contrast is between the church and the hostile Jewish leaders in *Das wahre Israel,* 61. K. Tagawa's analysis of the passage is even more precise and is in full agreement with the one presented here, "People and Community," 161–162.

6. Tagawa, "People and Community," 161.

21:5. The traditional story of the entry of Jesus in Jerusalem, into which this text is inserted in Matthew as a fulfillment citation, has been reworked in order to conform to the citation. The reworking is apparent in the stress on two animals, the ass and her colt, both in the verses preceding the citation and in the verse following the citation.

> "Go into the village opposite you, and immediately you will find an ass tied, *and a colt with her*; untie them and bring them to me. . . . This took place to fulfill what was spoken by the prophet, saying,
> "Tell the daughter of Zion,
> Behold, your king is coming to you,
> humble, and mounted on an ass,
> *and on a colt*, the foal of an ass."
> The disciples went and did as Jesus had directed them; they brought the ass *and the colt*, and put their clothes on *them*, and he sat on *them* (21:2ff.).

Only in Matthew are there two animals involved, and only in Matthew does the citation text occur. The implication of the passage is that two animals were found, brought to Jesus, and he rode on both of them. This strange conception of the event rests on a literalistic reading of the Zechariah text and an ignoring of the *parallelismus membrorum* which is inherent in the Hebrew poetry.

It has been argued that Matthew did not know about parallelism in Hebrew poetry.[7] However, the freedom of other Jewish interpreters in dealing with similar couplets suggests that Matthew's position, though arbitrary in our eyes, is by no means unique.[8] It is necessary to distinguish between our critical understanding of the original meaning of the text and the possible uses of that text by rules of exegesis vastly different from our own.

But even when one has granted that Matthew's view of the two animals is not exegetically wrong in the first-century world, it is difficult to see a reason for this curious application. Stendahl thinks that Matthew is relying on an interpretive tradition which has already introduced the two animals.[9] This is possible, but not demonstrable. Since the analyses of the mid-point texts have demonstrated Matthew's own skill in exegetical twists, it is also possible that Matthew is responsible for the adaptation. At any rate it is apparent that the form of the text has influenced Matthew's construction of the surrounding story.[10]

7. Examples of the difficulty caused for the critics by the two animals may be seen in Allen (*Matthew*, 220) and McNeile (*Matthew*, 294–295).

8. O. Michel ("ὄνος", *TDNT*, V, 286–287) presents a concise discussion of the phenomena; see also Stendahl (*School*, 119).

9. Implied by McNeile (*Matthew*, 294); and urged by Stendahl (*School*, 119).

10. For the Synoptic Problem the natural suggestion is that Mt's form is secondary either to Mk or a tradition available to him. On the other hand, the tradition of securing the ass for Jesus to ride must have been connected with the Zech prophecy very early, if it is not the reason for the creation of the tradition, so that it may be argued that the tradition behind Mk and Lk included the citation.

A similar adaptation of the surrounding story to fit a fulfillment text occurs in the pericope telling of the remorse of Judas, Mt 27:3–10. The story of Judas' return of the 30 pieces of silver and the Sanhedrin's decision to use the money to buy the potter's field is developed in exact correspondence with the fulfillment citation from Zech 11:13.

> But the chief priests, taking *the pieces of silver,* said, "It is not lawful to put them into the treasury, since they are *blood money.*" So they took counsel, and bought with them *the potter's field,* to bury strangers in. Therefore, that field has been called the Field of Blood to this day (Mt 27:6–8).
>
> Then was fulfilled what had been spoken by the prophet Jeremiah, saying, "And they took *the thirty pieces of silver,* the price of *him on whom a price had been set* by some of the sons of Israel, and they gave them for the *potter's field,* as the Lord directed me" (27:9–10).

The close relation of the text to the details of the passage is obvious. It is highly likely that the text's details have been worked backward into the story.[11]

Like the Zech 9:9 text just discussed, this citation presents a major puzzle to the interpreter of Matthew. Here it is the mistaken ascription to Jeremiah. It has long been supposed that Jeremiah was confused with Zechariah because Matthew was thinking of Jeremiah's buying a field (Jer 32:6–9) and his visit to the potter (Jer 18:1–2).[12] However, the solution proposed by R. H. Gundry is far more cogent.[13] The passage in Jeremiah which recalls most clearly the Judas story is 19:1–13. There Jeremiah buys a potter's earthen flask, takes some of the elders and the priests, goes out to the valley of Hinnom, and there delivers a scathing rebuke to the Judeans for, among other things, having filled the valley with *the blood of innocents* (19:1–4). In this passage, as in Matthew, a change of name occurs. "This place shall no more be called Topheth, or the valley of the son of Hinnom, but the *valley of Slaughter.*" And both places are places of burial (19:11). This is an impressive series of parallels and it certainly suggests that the doubling of Jeremiah and Zechariah occurred because of the relationship to the content of the Matthean passage.

But why does Matthew ascribe the text to Jeremiah and then cite Zechariah? Gundry suggests that it is done because:

> Mt., then, sees two separate prophecies, one typical and one explicitly fulfilled in one event, and makes the ascription to Jer. because the manifestness of the quotation from Zech. and the lack of verbal resemblance to Jer. would cause the Jer.-side of the prophecies to be lost. The naming of one author in a composite allusion is not unknown elsewhere. For example, the allusive quotation in II Chron. 36:21 is verbally drawn from Lev. 26:34f., yet ascribed to "Jer." (25:12; 29:10), from which the number of years,

11. Stendahl (*School,* 122–124) discusses the way in which the text and the context have been woven together.

12. See for example, Stendahl, *School,* 122.

13. R. H. Gundry, *The Use of the Old Testament,* 122–127.

"seventy," is drawn. Also, it is a rabbinical practice to quote various persons under one name if a similarity existed between the characters or actions of the persons.[14]

Whether or not Gundry's explanation for the ascription is compelling (it seems stronger than any other proposed solution), he is surely right in pointing out that it is the Jer 19 passage which draws together the Judas story and the Zechariah text. His argument is further supported by the fact that this apparently glaring mistake has occurred in a place where one of the most intricate interweavings of text and context has occurred in all of Matthew's uses of the OT. This suggests that considerable care went into the formulation of the passage. In terms of this study, however the ascription to Jeremiah is explained, the molding of text and context is another example of Matthew's use of the OT which influences the surrounding material but does not serve as a mid-point text.

A final example of this may be seen in the citations in the birth narrative, Mt 1:18–2:23. The relationship of the OT texts to the structure of this passage is blurred by the fact that their roles are not uniform. Two of the citation texts are simple fulfillment texts which do nothing to carry the narrative along (Isa 7:14 as cited in 1:22–23, and Jer 31:15 as cited in 2:17–18). In two other instances, the citation texts serve both as fulfillment texts and as essential steps in the logic of the narrative. It is only through the citation of Hos 11:1 in 2:15 that the reader is given the clue to the similarity of the infancy of Jesus to that of Moses. The final citation of the narrative, difficult as it is to provide the OT text which it presupposes,[15] gives the only reason that can be found in the narrative for the choice of Nazareth as a new home rather than any other Galilean town. Finally, the citation of Mic 5:2 in 2:5–6 occurs in the conversation with the Magi and is spoken by the chief priests and the scribes. This is a remarkable situation in Matthew and shows that the text is integral to the story and that Matthew is, at the very least, not citing it as one of his own fulfillment texts.

In view of the connections between the fulfillment texts and the narrative, it is unlikely that the Matthean narrative ever existed without the fulfillment citations in 1:22–23, 2:15,17–18, and 23. But it is interesting that the one non-fulfillment citation of the passage occurs in 2:1–12, which is a unit in itself. It is quite probable that this narrative is the traditional nucleus from which the Matthean birth narrative has been developed.[16] Not only is this unit self-contained (its introduction is, "Now when Jesus was born in

14. Gundry, *The Use of the Old Testament*, 125.

15. A number of explanations have been given for the claim that, "He shall be called a Nazarene," is prophesied in the OT. The basic alternatives are that **Ναζωραῖος** in Mt stems from the נצר of Jesse promised in Isa 11:1, or from the נזיר of God from Jgs 13:5. A thorough discussion of the problems surrounding this citation is given by Stendahl, *School*, 103–104 and 198–199.

16. Bultmann does mention the independence of the story in 2:1–12 from the rest of the narrative but does not develop the suggestion (*History of the Synoptic Tradition*, 292–294).

Bethlehem of Judea in the days of Herod the king," and its conclusion is, "And being warned in a dream not to return to Herod, they departed to their own country by another way"), but the Matthean themes of Davidic sonship (this theme dominates all of Mt 1) and the parallel between Jesus and Moses (which dominates 2:13–23) are not even mentioned in the narrative.

The presence of Matthean motifs and fulfillment citations in the material around 2:1–12 and the absence of those elements in 2:1–12 strongly suggest that the story of the birth in Bethlehem has been taken up by Matthew from tradition. Furthermore, the tendency of Matthew, which was demonstrated in the mid-point analyses, to work forward to a text and then outward from the text comes into play here if the Bethlehem story is viewed as the central text. Here a tradition about the birth of Jesus plays the role of the middle term. Before it Matthew develops by the genealogy and the virgin birth story the theme of Jesus' Davidic sonship (cf. 1:20, "Joseph, son of David"). After the Bethlehem story Matthew works outward from the implied hostility of Herod (vs. 12, "And being *warned* in a dream not to return to Herod") to develop the motif of the parallel between Moses and Jesus.

If it is true that Matthew has used an element of the Jesus tradition as the middle term in the birth narrative, then his use of the *mid-point technique* is not limited to the OT source but is also one of the ways in which his mind works with *all* of his materials in formulating the gospel. The birth narrative citations confirm the view that Matthew can and does mold contexts to fit his use of the texts, and vice versa, but also helps to anchor the *mid-point* technique in the work of Matthew as a redactor of the tradition about Jesus.[16a]

One other passage deserves attention for the question of the possible formative influence of OT texts in the construction of Matthew. An extensive allusion to Isa 35:5–6 occurs in the answer Jesus gives to the question of the disciples of John "Are you he who is to come, or shall we look for another?" (Mt 11:3).

> Go and tell John what you hear and see: *the blind receive their sight* and the *lame walk*, lepers are cleansed and *the deaf hear*, and the dead are raised up, and the poor have good news preached to them. And blessed is he who takes no offense at me (Mt 11:4–5).

> Say to those who are of a fearful heart, "Be strong, fear not! Behold your God will come with vengeance, with the recompense of God. He will come and save you." Then the *eyes of the blind shall be opened*, and the *ears of the deaf unstopped;* then shall the *lame man leap like a hart*, and the tongue of the dumb sing for joy (Isa 35:5–6).

In the Isaianic promise the blind, the lame, the deaf, and the dumb are assured deliverance. In the answer to John, the blind, the lame, the lepers,

16a. This analysis of the birth narrative is, of course, not exhaustive since there are many other important themes and problems in the section. For a much more detailed literary analysis see especially C. T. Davis, "Traditional and Redaction in Matthew 1:18–2:23," *JBL* 90 (1971) 404–421.

the deaf, the dead, and the poor are those to whom Jesus has ministered. The similarity in the lists requires the conclusion that the answer of Jesus is a deliberate allusion to the Isaiah text. The differences require explanation.

A major part of the difficulty surrounding the passage rests in the origins of the answer to the disciples of John. The alternatives appear to be that the pericope is basically authentic Jesus tradition, that the statement alluding to Isa 35 is a Jesus tradition to which a framework has been added by the early church, or that the entire pericope stems from the theology of the early church.

Of these alternatives, the second can be best defended. If one were to claim that the whole pericope comes from the Jesus situation, the allusive answer would have to be taken as an answer to the question of John's disciples, "Are you the one who is to come?" That would mean that Jesus expected John, John's disciples, and his hearers to recognize him as Messiah because of his miraculous deeds.[17] There is no evidence, however, that there was an expectation that the Messiah would be a wonder-worker.[18] There is, on the other hand, firm evidence that Christianity developed a concept that Jesus had performed signs and wonders as Messianic works.[19] The application of Isa 35:5–6 to the specific acts of Jesus rather than the time of salvation best reflects an early church setting.[20] But it is possible, as Bultmann says, that "the saying is intended simply to take the colors of (Second) Isaiah and use them to paint a picture of the final blessedness which Jesus believed is now beginning, without any need to relate particular statements with particular events that have already happened."[21] Only in this light is the argument persuasive that the allusion to Isa 35 reflects a setting in Jesus' ministry.[22]

A major difficulty with the foregoing reconstruction stems from the differences between Isa 35:5–6 and the reply by Jesus. If the colors of Isaiah's promise of the time of salvation were all that Jesus wished to convey, why are the non-Isaianic elements in the statement? The Isaiah text does not mention the cleansing of lepers, the raising of the dead, or the preaching of good news to the poor. These additions to the allusion are specific; they point to things that have already happened; they focus attention not on the

17. Bultmann, *History of the Synoptic Tradition*, 23.

18. J. Klausner, *The Messianic Idea in Israel* (New York: The Macmillan Co., 1955), 206.

19. The conception of the works of the Messiah in the broad sense is found in the Gospel of John (especially in the debate over the Sabbath healing in Jn 5 and 7) and in Acts 2:22, "a man attested to you by God with mighty works and wonders and signs," as well as in the Synoptic tradition.

20. W. Manson's attempt to refute Bultmann and claim authenticity for the whole passage does not take into account the difference between hope for the time of salvation when wonders would take place and hope for the Messiah; but the two ideas were not one in early Judaism. Wm. Manson, *Jesus the Messiah* (Philadelphia: Westminster Press, 1946), 63.

21. Bultmann, *History of the Synoptic Tradition*, 123.

22. This logic is accepted, for instance, by G. Bornkamm in *Jesus of Nazareth*, trans. by I. and F. McCluskey with J. Robinson (New York: Harper and Row, 1960), 67.

promise of salvation but rather on the activities of Jesus. This problem raises the question of the relationship of the allusive answer to its context in Matthew.

The allusion to Isa 35:5–6 does not play a *mid-point* role. The section following this pericope takes up the question of the importance of John the Baptist and does not include any further mention of Jesus' mighty acts. So the primary question to be asked is whether there is a relationship between the allusion and the material which precedes it. Perhaps Jesus did not feel constrained to relate the Isaiah promise to specific acts that had already happened, but did Matthew, in using the tradition, feel that need?

Many critics have recognized that miracles corresponding to the allusions in 11:5 can be found in the material preceding ch. 11.[23]

> The blind receive their sight: Two blind men are healed in 9:27–31.
> The lame walk: In 8:5–13 a paralyzed servant is healed.
> Lepers are cleansed: A leper is healed in 8:1–4.
> The dead are raised up: The girl is raised from the dead in 9:18–26.
> The poor have good news preached to them: In 5:3 Jesus says, "Blessed are the poor in spirit."

Is it simply coincidental that of the six promises in 11:5, five are narrated in the preceding chapters of Matthew? The coincidence is increased when we realize that one Greek word means deaf, mute, and the deaf-mute (κωφός). Therefore the healing of the mute demoniac in 9:32–34 does not need to be twisted to fulfill the sixth promise, "the deaf hear." All of the promises of Matthew 11:5 can be found fulfilled in the preceding chapters. Has the text been shaped to fit the context, or has the context been shaped to fit the text?

On the side of the context having been shaped to fit the allusion stands the evidence of the parallel passage in Luke. There, although Luke has given the promise his own setting,[24] Luke presents the answer to John's disciples in precise parallel to that given in Matthew. This requires literary dependence and, on the basis of the two-document hypothesis, would suggest that both Matthew and Luke took the reply from their Q source. If so, then Matthew must have shaped chs. 8 and 9 so as to make 11:5 an answer which has already been demonstrated in the gospel.

There are, however, difficulties with this view. Had Matthew been deliberately preparing the reader to see the relationship between 11:5 and the preceding material, would he not have conformed the miracles more closely to the wording of the allusion? Why does he not mention that the paralytic is lame? Why is the dumb demoniac not also deaf?

23. A. H. McNeile mentions and dismisses the view of Wellhausen and of Holtzmann that the miracles in chs. 8–9 are made to conform to the list in 11:5, *St. Matthew*, 129.

24. Lk 7:21: "In that hour he cured many of diseases and plagues and evil spirits, and on many that were blind he bestowed sight."

The second difficulty comes in locating the Matthean work which conforms chs. 8–9 to the text. It was demonstrated in the midpoint analysis of 9:10–34 that the organizational principle of that passage was the priority of mercy over sacrifice in accord with Matthew's understanding of the Hosea text. The logical relationships could be seen. Similarly, in order to show that the miracle stories have been shaped to provide a prelude for 11:5, some sign of editorial work by Matthew producing the correspondence is necessary. There is little such evidence, if any, and it is thus unlikely that Matthew wrote chs. 8 and 9 with an eye toward resolving the difficulties of one who looks back to see when the promises in 11:5 have been fulfilled by Jesus.

The alternative is that the allusion has been shaped to fit the context. This is supported by the precision of the relationship of the non-Isaianic promises to the preceding material and the obscurity of the other connections. But the difficulty is similar to that of the former alternative. If Matthew was shaping the allusion, why didn't he make it correspond with the preceding material? Especially, why did he not cite the promise to the dumb from Isaiah rather than the one to the deaf? An answer might lie in the fact that Matthew is using a tradition in which the allusion was already made, by Jesus perhaps, to Isa 35, using all four parts: the blind, the deaf, the lame, and the dumb. In the transition to Greek tradition, even before Matthew, the parallel of deaf to dumb (the same Greek word in the same sentence) caused the latter to drop out, leaving blind, deaf, and lame. The tradition then was expanded by the cleansing of lepers (from the Jesus tradition) in order to maintain a four-part structure. If so, Matthew may have known of the saying in this form:

The blind receive their sight
  and the lame walk.

The lepers are cleansed
  and the deaf hear.

The lack of a conjunction before "lepers are cleansed" supports this view. The two lines are two parts of a parallel couplet. The final three phrases of the section are all connected to this unit paratactically and give the impression of being addenda. The raising of the dead and the preaching to the poor do not fit in a unit about the healing of specific diseases.[25] So it is possible to suggest that already in the tradition Matthew had a pericope, probably in the form of the question by John's disciples, which contained the allusion to Isa 35 with the healing of the lepers already in it. Realizing that all four promises could be seen as fulfilled in the foregoing material without too harsh a demand upon the imagination, Matthew expanded the allusion

25. This is not to imply that these are peculiarly Matthean ideas. The expectation of the resurrection at the day of salvation is firmly rooted in first-century Judaism. And the preaching of good news to the poor is a part of another Isaiah text which was messianically understood, Isa 61:1.

in accord with further elements from his preceding material.[26] One of those elements, "preaching to the poor," helps him incorporate another allusion to Isaiah into the passage.

A firm decision in favor of one or the other of the alternatives is impossible. But Mt 11:5 does reflect the preceding material in a way not paralleled in Luke. Either Matthew shaped the context to fit the Isaiah text, or the text was shaped to fit the context. In either case, the passage is a further indication of the close formal relationship between the gospel material and the OT, a relationship which Matthew develops in various ways.

The study of non-mid-point citations and allusions to the OT in Matthew has produced the following results:

1. It is apparent that the use of the OT by Matthew varies considerably from instance to instance. It is not the case that every OT text is introduced by Matthew. Even when he introduces the text, Matthew does not always make extensive use of the text in molding the surrounding context.

2. In a considerable number of cases Matthew does use his special understanding of the OT texts to help him construct the passages around the texts. The actual influence of the text must be determined in each case.

3. The study of the birth narrative reveals that the mid-point technique is not limited to Matthew's use of the OT. He is also capable of using a tradition about Jesus as the logical center of a mid-point construction.

These results confirm and strengthen conclusions drawn about Matthew in the preceding chapter. The subtlety of the application of the OT texts, and the consistent use of them in contexts readily suited to a Jewish-Christian context, testify to Matthew's Jewish-Christian orientation. These same indications suggest that the "scribe trained for the kingdom of heaven" is an appropriate appellation for Matthew. His knowledge of both the OT and of Jewish traditions of its interpretation shows at least some exposure by Matthew to scribal training. However, Matthew works consistently in the interest of his understanding of the Christian faith. In doing so, he transforms the concept of a Jewish scribe into a Christian one by writing a gospel.

26. This reconstruction would virtually force a decision that Lk is secondary to Mt and in this passage literarily dependent. However, the composite literary form of the allusion must be explained even if one believes it stood in Q. The suggestion made above about the form of the allusion from which Mt may have worked fits Bultmann's view of the history of this tradition much better than the saying does as it now stands. Lk's form, in which two series of three elements each are paralleled, helps to overcome the clumsiness of the Matthean form but it obscures the relationship to Isa 35, and the joining of the last three elements, the deaf, the dead, and the poor, can scarcely reflect Semitic parallelism, for the two series are too different in content.

CHAPTER 4

PERICOPES MODELED ON OLD TESTAMENT PASSAGES

In the preceding chapters, the search for a redactional key for the work of Matthew has centered around his use of the OT. Uses of this source have been discovered in Matthew through examination of direct citations of the OT and unmistakable allusions to it. Of these uses, only certain examples have been helpful in establishing the work of Matthew. From the cases where evidence of Matthew's work could be detected and shown, however, considerable information was derived. The texts provided a key to the construction of the *mid-point* passages. The Matthean work with the OT texts and their contexts revealed a consistency of Jewish-Christian motifs and arguments which firmly locate the author as a Jewish-Christian.

Another avenue of approach through the use of a source remains unexplored. It is possible that the formulative ideas, or the narrative structure, or the elements of any given gospel pericope may be constructed on the model of an OT passage. In such an instance, there might be no direct citation of the OT passage and only minimal allusion, and yet the pericope could still owe its structure to the deliberate modeling on the basis of the OT story.

The examination of this type of modeling allusion is one which must be done with great caution for two reasons. First, there has been a tendency on the part of some interpreters to find an OT allusion for almost everything in the NT, and especially in Matthew. Since such a tendency can be pressed to absurdity, one primary requirement of an investigation seeking evidence of modeled passages is that exact and fairly extensive evidence in the NT text of the underlying OT passage is necessary. Moreover, on the basis of the proposed redactional method, a simple identification of individual allusions to the OT is insufficient evidence to support the claim that the OT passage is the literary basis of the NT passage. Rather, the allusions must in every case be shown to have a cumulative logical relationship to the structure of the passage itself. No ironclad rule stating the extent of logical and literary correspondence between the OT model and the pericope can be given. But in view of the difficulty mentioned above, it is advisable to require rather extensive evidence of the influence of the OT passage.

The detection of a definite connection between an OT and a NT passage does not establish that the connection is the work of the author of the NT document. It is possible for such a connection to belong to the preliterary stage of the tradition or to the source used by the writer. Therefore, the requirements for establishing the work of the redactor apply here as previously. There must be a combination of intrinsic logical structure and stylistic evidence before the passage can be assigned to the evangelist.

With these reservations in mind, the next analyses are directed to some passages in Matthew where there is a strong possibility that an OT passage has heavily influenced the form and content of the pericopes. The selection of these particular passages does not imply exhaustive coverage of the possibilities. Detection of the parallels is difficult and there may be other examples, in Matthew and elsewhere, of this type of relationship between the OT and the NT.

ANALYSIS 1: THE STILLING OF THE STORM— MT 8:23-27

The exegetical tradition in regard to this pericope is curious. It was early decreed by Wellhausen[1] and Weiss[2] that, although the story may be partially reminiscent of the Jonah story, its origins are not to be found there. More recently Taylor has reaffirmed this position.[3] Bultmann, however, introduced a novel twist. After arguing that there is no transfer of OT miracles to the NT in a literary sense,[4] he finds the closest parallel to this narrative in a Jewish story of a stilling by a Jewish boy at sea on a heathen boat, a story which Bultmann thinks is dependent on the Jonah story.[5] In all of this discussion no attempt has been made to present a systematic statement of the parallels between the story of Jonah in Jon 1 and the stilling on the Sea of Galilee in the Synoptics. A listing of the parallels is revealing:

Jonah 1	Stilling of the Storm
1. Departure by boat	1. Departure by boat
2. A violent storm at sea	2. A violent storm at sea
3. A sleeping main character	3. A sleeping main character
4. Badly frightened sailors	4. Badly frightened sailors
5. A miraculous stilling related to the main character	5. A miraculous stilling related to the main character
6. A marveling response by the sailors	6. A marveling response by the sailors

This is a striking set of parallels. It encompasses every important feature of the development of the two stories. In this light the denial of direct relationship between the Synoptic story (all 3 have all 6 elements) and the Jonah story is impossible. But there are important differences between the two stories. Unlike Jonah, Jesus is not fleeing from God. Jesus himself,

1. J. Wellhausen, *Das Evangelium Marci* (Berlin: 1909), 37.
2. J. Weiss, *Das älteste Evangelium* (Göttingen: Vandenhoeck and Ruprecht, 1903), 182f.
3. V. Taylor, *St. Mark*, 273.
4. R. Bultmann, *History of the Synoptic Tradition*, 230.
5. Bultmann, *History of the Synoptic Tradition*, 234–235.

rather than God, is the agent of the stilling. The setting is the Sea of Galilee and not the Mediterranean. All of these differences are easily understood as adaptations of the story to a new setting in the life of Jesus at the Sea of Galilee. Moreover, not one of the six parallel elements could be omitted from the story and leave the message intact. There is strong evidence that the two stories are structurally related and that the Synoptic story is dependent on the Old Testament narrative for its structure.

One element in the logic of the stories confirms this view. The sleeping of Jonah through a storm in the hold of a seafaring ship is plausible and credible. But the sleeping of Jesus stretched out on the deck of a small fishing boat on the Sea of Galilee through a storm so violent as to imperil boat and crew is not at all credible. The transition of setting is nearly perfect, but this one item betrays the dependence of the Synoptic account on the Jonah story. Since it is precisely the sleeping element which is not present in the Jewish tales cited by Bultmann, the dependence on the Jonah story must therefore be direct and literary.[6]

The dependence of the Synoptic story on Jon 1 is logically demonstrable, fulfilling the criterion established above for such a relationship. The story is of further interest because none of the Synoptic accounts is consistently closer than the others to the language of the Jonah story. Some examples in which each reflects the Jonah story more accurately than the others are:

Mt 8:24 *σεισμὸς μέγας ἐγένετο ἐν τῇ θαλάσσῃ*
Jon 1:4 MT ויהי סער גדול (סער = *σεισμός* not *ἄνεμος*)

Lk 8:22 *ἐνέβη*	Lk 8:23 *ἐκινδύνευον*
Jon 1:3 LXX *ἐνέβη*	Jon 1:4 LXX *ἐκινδύνευον*

Mk 4:41 *ἐφοβήθησαν φόβον μέγαν*
Jon 1:16 LXX *ἐφοβήθησαν φόβῳ μεγάλῳ*

It is difficult to ascertain just what this evidence means. But it is probable that the narrative *was already shaped* in accord with the Jonah story in the oral tradition. However, the literary parallels suggest that at least two and perhaps all three of the writers were aware of the dependence on the Jonah story and their variants reflect this knowledge. Or the varying parallels to the Jonah story could reflect variations of the story in the oral traditions available to the writers. The formal and literary evidence of the allusions to the Jonah story does not provide us with valuable new information about the relationships between the Synoptic accounts but points to a pre-Synoptic formation of the story based on the Jonah story.

6. This is an important challenge to Bultmann's view that the oral transmission of the Jesus stories was completely divorced from literary relationship to the OT. This is a curious limitation for a tradition which he believes to have originated in a Palestinian milieu (*History of the Synoptic Tradition,* 240). Both an oral and a literary familiarity with the Jon story could be presupposed in that milieu.

What can be learned of Matthean redaction from the story? This is the question which has been discussed by Bornkamm.[7] He has seen that, while the catch-word *follow* (ἀκολουθεῖν) is the most obvious means by which the pericope is attached to what precedes, the meaning of *follow* is to be understood by the immediately preceding verses, which are concerned with the radical claim of discipleship (Mt 8:18–21). Even more important from Matthew's perspective is the use of the word Lord (κύριε) in the prayer-like request of the disciples which links the story to the preceding material. Both of these elements are peculiar to Matthew.[8] The first belongs to Matthew's own introduction of the story; the second is so apropos to the story both in the request for control over nature and in the reminiscence of the saving power of Yahweh over nature that it is difficult to determine whether Matthew has introduced the word or used the story here because of its connection with the preceding stories.[9]

What Matthew has done with the tradition is clear. In 7:29 the crowds have marveled "for he taught them as one who had authority, and not as their scribes." Then in 8:2,6,8,21 the word used by persons addressing Jesus is *kyrie* and not *teacher*. This sets the stage for the story in which Jesus is shown to have the wonderful power of the *kyrios*. The theme which underlies the section is that of discipleship. Following Jesus as Lord requires a deeper and more radical trust than just following him as teacher (in 8:26, Jesus berates the frightened disciples as *little-faiths*). By the marveling response of "the men" (8:27) rather than just the disciples, Matthew makes the story relate to the disciples and to the wider situation of the church of his own day as well.[10]

This means that the allusions to Jon 1 by which the Synoptic story is framed are not primarily the work of Matthew. Matthew has employed the story in order to demonstrate that the discipleship which Jesus requires is that of a man toward his Lord. For purposes of the present study *the negative result is very important.* A Matthean pericope has been found which is modeled on an OT story. But the redactional work of Matthew resides in his use of the story rather than in his construction of it. One hurdle has been cleared. There is evidence for the existence of a NT passage modeled on an OT passage. But the hurdle cleared establishes another. The technique of modeling is not Matthew's alone.

7. G. Bornkamm, "The Stilling of the Storm in Matthew," in *Tradition and Interpretation in Matthew*, 52–57.

8. Bornkamm, "Stilling of the Storm," 54–55.

9. Bornkamm assumes the priority of Mk and so does not discuss the aptness of κύριε to the original story. The point should be raised, however, and an unbiased assessment suggests that perhaps the term was in the tradition Mt used.

10. This picture of the redactional activity of Mt is in essential agreement with Bornkamm, *op cit.*, except that here the rationale of lordship is connected to the attitude of the crowd in 7:29.

ANALYSIS 2: MATTHEW'S TRANSFIGURATION NARRATIVE AND SINAI

It has long been suspected that allusion to the traditions about Moses on Sinai lies behind the Synoptic accounts of the transfiguration of Jesus (Mt 17:1–9; Mk 9:2–10; Lk 9:28–36). Certain elements of the story make this suggestion quite natural: the ascent of the mountain, the shining of Jesus' clothing (and face in Mt/Lk), the cloud, and the voice. The influence of the Sinai accounts on the story has not been adequately treated, however, especially in the two most popular theories of the origin of the story, namely, the view that the account is a post-resurrection experience projected into the life of Jesus and the opinion that it is a symbolic narrative made up of two distinct strands, a Hellenistic metamorphosis of the divine man and a Jewish-Christian presentation of Jesus as the Messiah.[11] A further discussion of the structure of the passage is needed.

In *The Setting of the Sermon on the Mount*, W. D. Davies takes up the question of the New Moses motif in Matthew's presentation of Jesus and its relevance to this pericope.[12] A brief review of the evidence he has marshalled as parallels between the Sinai accounts and the Synoptic stories will provide a basis for a more precise analysis in line with the method of inquiry which is being tested in this study.

Signs of the Sinai event in the Marcan account:[13]

1) Mk 9:2—"after six days" corresponds to "on the seventh day" of the theophany to Moses, Ex 24:16.
2) Mk 9:7—the voice speaks from the cloud as in Ex 24:16.
3) Mk 9:2—Peter, James and John parallel Moses' companions, Aaron, Nadab, and Abihu, Ex 24:1.
4) Mk 9:2–3—the radiance of Jesus compares with that of Moses' radiance upon descent from Sinai, Ex 34:29ff.
5) Mk 9:4—the two figures who appear with Jesus, Moses and Elijah, are the only two in the OT tradition to confer with God on Sinai; Moses in Ex 24 and 34, Elijah in 1 Kgs 19:9–13.
6) Mk 9:7—"hear him" is reminiscent of the authority of Moses and of the promise of a prophet like Moses, "him you shall heed," of Dt 18:15.

11. For the view that the story reflects a post-resurrection appearance see Bultmann, *History of the Synoptic Tradition*, 259–261. The double origin position is held by E. Lohmeyer. "Die Verklärung Jesu nach dem Markusevangelium," *ZNW* 16 (1922) 185–215.

12. Davies, *The Setting of the Sermon on the Mount*, 50–55.

13. Davies, *The Setting of the Sermon on the Mount*, 50, presents these parallels in similar fashion.

The objection of Bultmann that some of these items are the common stock of theophanic traditions does not suffice to explain the number of parallels to one specific theophany, Ex 24 and 34. The setting is the same, the principal characters are parallel, the natural phenomena are the same, and the timing is the same.[14] The last point illustrates the importance of the details. It is impossible to give a reason for the reference to *after six days* in terms of the narrative structure in either Mark or Matthew.[15] There is no such chronological note in any of the accounts of post-Easter appearances. The facts that the detail fits with several others in reference to a limited passage in the OT and that that passage is one of vital importance to first-century Judaism suggest that the story is consciously shaped in reference to the theophany at Sinai.[16]

Although the parallels to Sinai are present in Mark, there is no emphasis on these allusions in Mark's presentation. Mark himself is far more concerned with the picture of Jesus as the Suffering Messiah and even places Elijah ahead of Moses. Mark has used the story to point toward the suffering of Jesus, but his editorial work has not obscured all of the allusions to the Exodus story.

In Luke the allusions are preserved and are even heightened as compared to Mark *even though* Luke understands *the glory* of Jesus, Moses, and Elijah as that of heavenly beings and not as the overshadowing glory (Shekinah) of the Lord. For Luke the story is a prefiguration of the ascension and exaltation. Moses and Elijah speak of the departure of Jesus (ἔξοδος) which he was about to accomplish in Jerusalem. This reference does not point to the crucifixion but to the ascension, Acts 1:6–11, when Jesus takes his rightful place in glory in heaven with such figures as Moses and Elijah. Thus Luke uses the story of the transfiguration to point to Jesus' heavenly role and destiny and not to emphasize the earthly mission. Yet he leaves all of the major elements of the tradition intact.

In Matthew the climactic incident of the story is the voice from the cloud, not the conversation with Moses and Elijah. These three, according to Matthew, share in the rare privilege of having the glory surround them on Sinai with God speaking favorably of them. Moses was commissioned to teach Israel the law, Ex 25:1ff.; Elijah was commissioned to anoint Jehu, 1 Kgs 19:16; and Jesus is commissioned as the teacher of the disciples, Mt 17:5, "This is my beloved son, with whom I am well pleased; *listen to him.*" The last phrase makes a direct connection between Jesus and the promised prophet like Moses of Dt 18:15, "him you shall heed." Thus Matthew's use of the story is firmly in line with the Sinai/Moses allusions of the narrative.

In Matthew the story is not as neatly dovetailed into its context as it is in

14. Bultmann, *History of the Synoptic Tradition,* 260.

15. Bultmann, 259, where he makes no mention of the Sinai event.

16. The delivery of the law at Sinai forms the basis of Pharisaic Judaism (*Pirke Aboth 1:1*).

Mark and Luke. Davies says, "It would seem that Matthew, after relating the Transfiguration, cannot quickly enough get to the discourse section, giving teaching of Jesus, in 17:24–18:35."[17] The connection to the Elijah question is awkward.

> And as they were coming down the mountain, Jesus commanded them, "Tell no one the vision, until the Son of man is raised from the dead." And the disciples asked him, "Then why do the scribes say that first Elijah must come?" (Mt 17:9–10).

Actually there is a break between vss. 9 and 10 and the two passages probably are not intended to run together in this way. The injunction to silence closes the transfiguration story for Matthew. The Elijah motif, picked up in the disciples' question, connects the two pericopes, but the mention of Elijah in the transfiguration narrative does not provide a suitable introduction to the question or to the ensuing discussion.

The analysis has reached the following preliminary conclusions. 1) There is sufficient evidence, both cumulative and logical, to support the contention that the structure of the Synoptic transfiguration accounts rests on an allusion to the experience of Moses on Sinai in Ex 24–34. 2) The story is woven into its immediate and general context more clearly in Mark and Luke than in Matthew. 3) On the other hand, the Moses/Sinai allusion is more extensive in Matthew and more appropriate to Matthew's use of the Mosaic theme.

How is this evidence to be assessed? Because of their adaptation of the story to their concerns and their lack of interest in either Sinai or Moses motifs, Mark and Luke may be ruled out as originators of the story. They take it up from tradition available to them. The extensive nature of the allusions and the use elsewhere in Matthew's gospel of mountain and Moses motifs might suggest that Matthew created the story. The negative evidence is not so strong here as for Mark and Luke, but some exists. Had Matthew created the story, would he have left it so unrelated to its present context as it now stands? The evidence gained about Matthew's creativity in the analyses suggests his skill at coupling and connecting stories and sections. More significantly, signs of Matthean language are meager in the passage. The adjustment of the words spoken by the voice from heaven to those of the voice at the baptism is probably due to Matthew but of minor importance. The double use of "and behold" as a conjunction in vss. 3 and 5 is also a minor narrative adjustment to the author's style. Other than that it is difficult to say that the language or ideas of the pericope are Matthew's.

As a result of this appraisal, the only judgment that may be reached regarding the origin of the pericope is that it probably is a pre-Synoptic tradition which took shape in Jewish-Christianity as a legitimation of the authority vested in Jesus' teaching by Christians. Matthew has altered the

17. Davies, *Setting*, 53.

tradition the least, Mark the most, and Luke's version represents a midway approach. Part of the literary evidence within the pericope suggests that Matthew and Luke are here independent of Mark. It does not prove Mark's dependence on Matthew or Luke or clarify their relationship to one another. That Matthew values the tradition highly and uses it in its original sense is nearly certain; that Matthew created the narrative himself is unlikely. (This would remain true even if Mark and Luke could be shown to have used the Matthean story as the basis of their accounts.)

The search for a Matthean pericope modeled on an OT passage has again reached a positive and negative result. The positive result is form-critical in nature. The evidence is strong that the transfiguration narrative is constructed by allusion to the Sinai theophany, Ex 24–34, and related texts, 1 Kgs 19:9–18 and Dt 18:15. The passage is an instance of a NT pericope modeled on an OT passage.

The negative result concerns the work of Matthew. As in the previous analysis, though the evidence is strong that Matthew is in full accord with the transfiguration tradition available to him, there is little or no evidence that his mind and style brought the story to existence. This story does, however, show that the modeling of stories about Jesus upon OT passages is a practice primarily suited to a Jewish-Christian milieu. Such passages serve best when the allusions are recognized by the reader (or hearer) and provide the intended connection between his hopes for a Messiah and Jesus proclaimed as Messiah. So the search for a modeling use of the OT has been partially successful. The OT is used this way in Matthew's gospel. But these passages come to Matthew from his Jewish-Christian tradition, with which he is in fundamental agreement.

ANALYSIS 3: THE MATTHEAN CRUCIFIXION NARRATIVE

That all of the gospel accounts of the crucifixion of Jesus have been influenced in some measure by the early Christian use of Ps 22 is widely recognized.[18] Of the four narratives, those in Matthew and Mark make the most extensive use of the psalm. Luke and John present versions which differ greatly from each other and from the Mt/Mk account. The role of Ps 22 in the structure of the Matthean narrative is the primary topic for consideration here. To discover that role, an appraisal of the allusions to Ps 22 in Mt 27 must be made.

The influence of Ps 22 in Matthew's passion narrative is limited to the story of the crucifixion, Mt 27:26–46. The allusions and references to Ps 22 in this passage are as follows:

1) Mt 27:27—Then the soldiers of the governor took Jesus into the praetorium and they gathered the whole (ὅλος) battalion before (ἐπί)[19] him.

18. See for example, Lindars, *New Testament Apologetic*, 89–93.
19. ἐπί here probably has the force of *against*, cf. Bauer-Arndt-Gingrich, *Lexicon*, 288.

Ps 22:16—Yea, dogs are round about me; a company of evildoers encircle me.

Although this allusion has not been previously recognized, there are strong reasons for believing that it is one. The two qualifying phrases related to the soldiers are important. "Of the governor" makes clear the Roman rather than Jewish make-up of the group. "The whole battalion" (*ὅλην τὴν σπεῖραν*) emphasizes the gathering of the company. That a gathering of Roman soldiers would be a company of evildoers in Jewish eyes is axiomatic. But that the entire company would be mustered for the mockery of a condemned prisoner is very unlikely (the gathering of the "whole company" occurs only in the Mt/Mk version of the story, contrast Lk 23:24; Jn 19:1).[20] The fact that the term *dog* (*κύων* or כלב) was used by Jews as an epithet for Gentiles and especially for the Romans[21] makes the presence of an allusion probable. When this is considered alongside the cumulative evidence of the following allusions, it gains considerable strength.

2) Mt 27:35—they divided his garments among them by casting lots.

Ps 22:18—they divide my garments among them, and for my raiment they cast lots.

That this is a deliberate allusion to the psalm is self-evident.

3) Mt 27:39—And those who passed by derided him, wagging their heads, and saying. . . .

Ps 22:7—All who see me mock at me, they make mouths at me, they wag their heads.

This allusion is also deliberate. The use of the exact motion of the passers-by is so explicit as to make the allusive connection certain. The allusion is buttressed in another way. Not only do the soldiers and passers-by mock Jesus, but also the two thieves. This reinforces the allusion to the words of the psalm, "all who see me mock at me."

4) Mt 27:43—He trusts in God; let God deliver him now, if he desires him. . . .

Ps 22:8—He committed his cause to the Lord; let him deliver him, let him rescue him, for he delights in him.

This allusion occurs in the midst of several different accusations against Jesus which are placed in the mouths of the Jewish authorities and is another direct reference to the plight of the sufferer of the psalm.

5) Mt 27:46—And about the ninth hour Jesus cried with a loud voice, "Eli, Eli, lama sabachthani?" that is, "My God, my God, why hast thou forsaken me?"

Ps 22:1—My God, my God, why hast thou forsaken me?

20. In both Mk and Mt the reference to the gathering of the whole company is redundant. Taylor smooths over the implausibility of the mustering of 200 to 600 men by saying, "The phrase is used loosely for those who were available at the time" (*St Mark*, 585). This is an interpretive conjecture dependent upon the view that the reporting is historically reliable.

21. For this use of the word dog to characterize *goyim* see Strack-Billerbeck, I, 447, 723–726; Bauer-Arndt-Gingrich, *Lexicon*, 462.

The reference is again unmistakable. Although Matthew conforms the name of God to the Hebrew, the text of the transliteration is mixed and probably has been adjusted to the Elijah discussion which follows. It affords little help concerning which OT text tradition is being followed.[22] Since all of the other allusions are possible through either the MT or LXX, the question of the language of the OT text is not pertinent for the problem of the allusions.

These five connections between the Matthean crucifixion narrative and Ps 22 present a strong initial case for supposing that at least part of the structure of the narrative derives from the paralleling of Jesus with the sufferer of Ps 22:1–21. Moreover, Matthew is the only author to express all five allusions so clearly (the allusion to "the dogs" is best seen in the Matthean version of the narrative).[23]

Why should so extensive a set of parallels have been drawn between the crucifixion narrative and Ps 22? It has often been maintained that this psalm was viewed as a gold mine of references to the righteous sufferer.[24] Although this is an attractive hypothesis, it needs support within the narrative. But there is no mention of innocent suffering in the Matthean crucifixion narrative and no hint of it in the specific allusions used. In fact, it is Luke who stresses just this theme of innocent suffering, but does it without reference to Ps 22.[25] The Psalm itself does not speak of the suffering of an innocent person but only of one who "committed his cause to the Lord," (Ps 22:8). Not a word is said in the Matthean crucifixion narrative itself of the innocence of Jesus. There is no sound internal evidence to connect the theme of the righteous sufferer with the use of Ps 22 in the passion narrative.

If the attractive hypothesis proves to be without foundation in the text, an alternate must be sought. If Ps 22 is not used as model of the righteous sufferer, then how is it employed? Asking this question of the Matthean narrative leads to a new road of insight.

Allusions to Ps 22 occur in four basic places in Matthew's crucifixion narrative: 1) in the mocking of Jesus by Roman soldiers, 2) in the dividing of the garments immediately after the crucifixion, 3) in the mocking of Jesus by the passers-by and Jewish leaders, and 4) in the cry of despair by Jesus. In the first three of these scenes, another motif is always present. In each of them Jesus is declared crucified as "king" of the Jews or of Israel. The soldiers dress Jesus as a king and mock him saying, "Hail, King of the Jews."

22. Stendahl, *School*, 83–87.

23. Mk does not stress the fact that the soldiers were Roman or make so pointed a reference to the gathering of the whole company in hostility, Mk 15:16.

24. Lindars, *New Testament Apologetic*, 90–91. It is true that in Mt Jesus' innocence is established in the scene before Pilate. Even there Jesus is, in Pilate's words, "who is called Christ." The charge against Jesus is thus not denied by Mt.

25. Where Lk establishes the innocence of Jesus (in the conversation between the thieves, 23:39–43) no allusions to Ps 22 occur.

The soldiers nail above his head the charge, "This is Jesus the King of the Jews," immediately after dividing the garments. The mocking Jewish leaders say, "He is the King of Israel; let him come down now from the cross," and "for he said, 'I am the Son of God.'" Therefore, it is clear that the allusions to Ps 22 which lead to the climactic cry of dereliction are deliberately juxtaposed to references to Jesus as the dying Messiah-King.[26] The evidence for the interweaving of these motifs may best be seen by means of the following chart which underlines the close conjunction of the two themes.

THE STRUCTURE OF THE MATTHEAN CRUCIFIXION NARRATIVE

References to Jesus as "the King"	From the Narrative, Mt 27:26–46	From Ps 22
SYMBOLICALLY IN THE DRESSING UP OF JESUS VERBALLY IN THE MOCKING WORDS	27–29 Then *the soldiers of the governor* took Jesus into the praetorium, and they *gathered the whole battalion before him.* And they stripped him and put A SCARLET ROBE upon him, and plaiting A CROWN of thorns they put it on his head, and put a REED IN HIS RIGHT HAND. And KNEELING BEFORE HIM they mocked him, saying, "HAIL, KING OF THE JEWS!"	16 Yea, *dogs* are round about me; *a company of evildoers encircle me.*
IN THE CHARGE ABOVE HIS HEAD	35–37 And when they had crucified him *they divided his garments among them by casting lots. . . .* And over his head they placed the charge against him, "THIS IS JESUS THE KING OF THE JEWS."	18 *They divide my garments among them, and for my raiment they cast lots.*
IN THE MOCKING OF THE BYSTANDERS	39–41 And *those who passed by derided* him, *wagging their heads* and saying, ". . . ." So *also the chief priests, with the scribes and elders, mocked* him, saying, "He saved others; he cannot save himself. HE IS THE KING OF ISRAEL; let him come down now from the cross, and we	7 *All who see me mock* at me, they make mouths at me, *they wag their heads;*

26. The title *Son of God* is not solely Davidic in Mt. This has been made clear in the transfiguration narrative. But in the mouths of the Jewish opponents it is best understood as a reiteration of *King of Israel.*

References to Jesus as "the King"	From the Narrative, Mt 27:26-46	From Ps 22
Possible allusion	will believe in him. *He trusts in God; let God deliver him now, if he desires him;* for he said, 'I AM THE SON OF GOD.'" *And the robbers who were crucified with him* also *reviled* him in the same way.	8 *"He committed his cause to the Lord; let him now deliver him,* let him rescue him, *for he delights in him!"*
	46 And about the ninth hour Jesus cried with a loud voice, *"Eli, Eli, lama sabachthani?"* that is, *"My God, my God, why hast thou forsaken me?"*	1 (MT) *My God, my God, why hast thou forsaken me?*

Allusions are indicated in italics or heavy print. The allusive reference is definite unless it is underscored; underscoring indicates a more oblique allusion.

That a connection exists within the narrative between the allusive use of Ps 22 and the motif of the crucified king is now apparent. But why does this connection exist? One way of answering this might be by supposing that Ps 22 was remembered, even in the days of the Second Temple, as a royal lament. Such a position is precarious, however, because the evidence for such a use of the psalm is not sure for its original setting, much less for the period of the Second Temple.[27] Instead, most contemporary scholars would argue that Ps 22 presents an individual lament in both form and content.[28] But even those who choose this line of reasoning must deal with elements in the psalm that point to perspectives beyond the individual. The adversaries in vss. 12–21 are symbolic of forces overwhelming the plaintiff, forces more than personal ills and trials, national or even cosmic.[29] The hymn of victory in vss. 25–31 moves from the individual to the nations and to posterity, all

27. Scholarly debate on the possibilities of parallels to Babylonian or Canaanite renewal rituals is intense. Among the studies are those by A. Bentzen, *King and Messiah* (Napierville, Ill.: A. R. Allenson, 1954); I. Engnell, *Studies in Divine Kingship in the Ancient Near East* (2nd ed.; Oxford: Blackwell's, 1967); and S. Mowinckel, *He That Cometh,* trans. by G. W. Anderson (New York: Abingdon Press, 1954).

28. H. Gese provides a concise statement of this exegesis of Ps 22 in "Psalm 22 und das Neue Testament," *ZTK* 65 (1968) 1–22. See also C. Westermann, *The Praise of God in the Psalms,* trans. K. R. Crim (Philadelphia: John Knox Press, 1965), 64–81.

29. See Gese, "Psalm 22," 10–14.

joined in praise of God. This combination of individual lament and communal praise is important for a grasp of the NT use of the psalm.

For the first-century Christian, Ps 22 has another feature which relates it to kingship; it was accepted in NT times as a psalm of David. The application of several of the psalms to Jesus is common in early Christian apologetic, especially Ps 110, which was also regarded as a psalm of David.[30] In the search for a justification of the crucifixion of the one they called Messiah, Ps 22 offered great help.

Hartmut Gese has attempted to show that the psalm was originally apocalyptic in its orientation and had inherent within it a death/resurrection motif.[31] Since evidence of the use of Ps 22 in apocalyptic circles other than the NT is lacking, this suggestion must be taken only as an attractive hypothesis. But it may be agreed that Gese is right in sensing that the *whole* psalm is in the thought of the Christians who use it.[32] He argues that the use of the psalm in relation to Jesus' death is intrinsically eschatological. The story of Jesus' death gives meaning to the Christian eucharist. The humiliation of Jesus on the cross is the sure first step of the drama of salvation that unfolds in the psalm. What Gese does not note is the combination of Messianic language alongside the use of Ps 22 in the narrative of Jesus' death.[33] Whoever the individual of the lament may originally have been intended to be is thus irrelevant. For Christians this psalm of David prefigures the death of Jesus the Messiah, the son of David, in a prelude to his victory.[34]

In this way all of Ps 22, and not simply the lament section, was understood as a psalm of David which spoke appropriately of the situation of Jesus' dying on the cross, his being delivered, and then his exaltation in the resurrection. The cry of desolation which utilizes Ps 22:1 is bolstered by other allusions to the psalm in support of the affirmation that Jesus, who suffered the cross in humiliation and mockery, is the true Messiah King, the Son of David, now raised to victory in the resurrection. The reason for the surprising combination of the kingship motif with the psalm is made clear by the combination of Ps 22 allusions and references to Jesus as "King."

In the crucifixion narrative only the lament section is appropriate. But that Matthew and his fellow Christians would see the latter part of the psalm fulfilled in Jesus' resurrection and in his impending return as *king* can be

30. Lindars, *New Testament Apologetic,* 45–51.

31. Gese, "Psalm 22," 13–17.

32. Gese says, "Dieser Bezug auf Ps. 22 beschränkt sich nicht auf die zitierten Eingangsworte des Psalmes. Es ist ja von vornherein wahrscheinlich, dass das Zitat des Psalmanfangs den ganzen Psalm meint." "Psalm 22," 1.

33. Gese, "Psalm 22," 14–22.

34. In spite of the sentence quoted in footnote 32 above, Gese restricts his consideration of the role of Ps 22 in the narrative to the cry (14–17). He even says that the interpretation of Jesus' death has nothing to do with the Messiah (17).

seen by paralleling other Matthean passages to the words of the closing verses of the psalm.

> For dominion belongs to the Lord and he rules over the nations Ps 22:28.
>
> When the Son of man comes in his glory, and all the angels with him, then he will sit on his glorious throne. Before him will be gathered all the nations. . . . Then the King will say . . . Mt 25:31ff.
>
> Men shall tell of the Lord to the coming generation, and proclaim his deliverance to a people yet unborn, that he has wrought it Ps 22:30f.
>
> All authority in heaven and on earth has been given to me. Go therefore and make disciples of all nations . . . Mt 28:18–19.

The crucifixion has been understood as a part of God's plan for the Messiah, a plan which leads through humiliation and death to glory and power. It can be no accident that a psalm is used to tell of Jesus' death, which presents the same duality and is also a psalm of David.

Further support is available for this understanding of the construction of the narrative from the situation of Jewish-Christianity. As late as Justin Martyr's *Dialogue with Trypho* the crucifixion of Jesus was one of the major barriers to Jewish acceptance of Jesus as Messiah.[35] This barrier is also clear in Paul (1 Cor 1:23). In the light of the Jewish objection to a man who had been crucified by the Romans being proclaimed Messiah, the Matthean narrative is a theological construction accepting the scandal of the cross by using Ps 22. The messiahship of Jesus is an important theme for Matthew (the theme recurs in the genealogy, the birth narratives, the Beelzebul controversy, and the triumphal entry). Matthew also stresses more than the other evangelists the kingship of the risen and returning Jesus.[36] The use of Ps 22 to confront the scandal of the cross and to affirm the messiahship of Jesus is clear from the literary evidence within the narrative and from the historical situation which it suits so well.

It is likely that the Matthean crucifixion narrative was constructed by someone who, among other things, intended to provide a theological solution to the problem of the crucifixion of Jesus the Messiah. Was this person Matthew? It has already been shown that the manner of using the OT and the emphasis on the kingship of Jesus are in accord with the work of

35. Eng. trans. from *The Ante-Nicene Fathers*, I, ed. by Roberts and Donaldson (New York: Charles Scribner's Sons, 1925), 224, ch. xc; Trypho says, "But prove to us whether He must be crucified and die so disgracefully and so dishonorably by the death cursed in the law. For we cannot bring ourselves to think of this."

36. See J. A. T. Robinson, "The 'Parable' of the Sheep and the Goats," *NTS* 2 (1955–1956) 229–230 for a listing of Mt's uses of the king title in parabolic material where "the fact that the character is a king is fortuitous, if not otiose" (230): Mt 18:23; 22:7,11; 25:34,40. To these instances should be added other references to Jesus' Davidic origins, such as 1:1; 1:20; 2:2; 2:4; 9:27; 12:23. Also, the picture of "the Son of Man seated on his glorious throne" (19:28 and 25:34,40) shows how much the royal throne dominates Matthean Christology.

Matthew. Such evidence would offer some support for an argument for Matthew as the composer of the narrative. Matthean authorship is not well supported, however, by evidence of peculiarly Matthean language or style. There is nothing in the structure or style of the passage that is *so distinctively* Matthean that it proves Matthean composition. The parallels are so strong between Matthew and Mark in the narrative that literary dependence is certain. Therefore, several alternative solutions to the question of the origin of the narrative are possible.

The story could have originated with Matthew for the reasons already given. Matthew would have provided a theological defense of his belief that Jesus, though crucified, is the Messiah. But the evidence for so strong a claim for Matthean creativity is minimal, and full Matthean authorship is improbable.

Secondly, Matthew may have used Mark and have stressed the relationship of messiahship to Ps 22 in accord with his and his church's understanding and use of the crucifixion narrative. In this case, Mark is even less likely than Matthew to have created the narrative because Mark does not stress the Davidic Sonship or Messianic kingship of Jesus.

Another solution may be the use by both evangelists of a common tradition. Matthew was surely not the first Jewish-Christian to meditate upon the problem of the crucified Messiah. The telling of the crucifixion story may well have had its original setting in the eucharist of the Jewish-Christian community as Gese suggests.[37] The meal worship itself would have been an anticipation of the victory promised in Ps 22:22–31. The meal and the story of Jesus' death used with it would have served, as Paul says, to "proclaim the Lord's death until he comes" (1 Cor 11:26).

A primitive tradition behind Matthew and Mark may, in fact, be recoverable. The extensive theological adaptation of Ps 22 to the crucifixion narrative helps to rule out the view that this application came about as a result of a genuine historical reminiscence of the cry of dereliction by Jesus in the words of Ps 22:1. Not only is this cry absent from the Lucan and Johannine narratives, but a theological motivation for paralleling the crucifixion and Ps 22 has now been established.[38] But if Ps 22 does not provide the basis of the development, the kingship motif may. Firm support for the historicity of the fact that the charge against Jesus, "King of the Jews," was placed on the cross comes not only from all three of the accounts (cf. Lk 23:38; Jn 19:19), but from historical probability. As Paul Winter in his examination of the use of such inscriptions says:

> If anything that is recorded of his Passion in the Four Gospels accords with history, it is the report that he was crucified and that the cross that bore his tortured body also bore a

37. Gese, "Psalm 22," 17–21.

38. B. Lindars, *New Testament Apologetic,* 89, argued for the historicity of the cry because "it is in any case impossible to find a motive for inventing it." That can no longer be maintained in view of Gese's article and of this analysis.

summary statement of the cause for which he had been sentenced to the *servile supplicium*.[39]

The problem of the crucifixion of Jesus was always the problem both of his humiliating death and his death as King of the Jews. The messiahship of Jesus could only be maintained if the problem posed by the death of Jesus for political reasons could be resolved. Ps 22 was brought to bear on that problem in order to provide an effective solution.

A rudimentary narrative framework can be detected behind the present theologically oriented narrative in Matthew and Mark by simply deleting Ps 22 and messiahship motifs. It consists of the following elements:

1) Pilate turned Jesus over to the soldiers to be crucified: Mt 27:26/Mk 15:15.
2) Simon the Cyrenian was compelled to carry the cross: Mt 27:32/Mk 15:21.
3) Jesus was crucified: Mt 27:35/Mk 15:24.
4) The charge, "This is Jesus, King of the Jews," was placed on the cross: Mt 27:37/Mk 15:26.
5) Jesus died after a last loud cry: Mt 27:50/Mk 15:37.

Around these fundamental data the Jewish-Christian community developed its crucifixion narrative by weaving references to Ps 22 and to the humiliation of the Messiah into the story.[40] Perhaps the surest clue that this had happened is the fact that the mention of Simon carrying the cross could not be utilized in the theological rewriting of the death of the Messiah-King as prefigured in Ps 22 but it was nevertheless retained.

From this tradition, the narrative was probably developed in conjunction with Ps 22 at an early date. The Jewish-Christian modeling of the crucifixion narrative on Ps 22 lies behind the Matthew/Mark version of the narrative. While it coincides best with Matthew's redactional purposes and interests and is better preserved in Matthew, the evidence is insufficient to make a judgment on the literary relationship. Matthew may have adapted Mark's version in line with his own perception of the role of Ps 22 (or its use in this form in his church), or Mark may have used Matthew and slightly changed the structure for his own reasons. Most important for our inquiry into the role of the OT as an external source in Matthew is the high probability that the modeling of the crucifixion narrative on Ps 22 was *not done by Matthew first*, but belonged to his tradition.

39. Paul Winter, *On the Trial of Jesus* (Berlin: De Gruyter, 1961), 109.

40. While it seems probable that this occurred in Palestinian Jewish-Christianity, Gese ("Psalm 22," 14), errs in insisting that the absence of allusion to the "They have pierced my hands and feet" in Ps 22:16 LXX means that the background of the use of the psalm is the Aramaic. Not only is the Hebrew just as likely the background for the use of the psalm, but as Lindars has shown (*New Testament Apologetic*, 92), the LXX is obscure in itself at this point and may not have been read as a reference to crucifixion at all.

ANALYSIS 4: "THE GOOD IS ONE"—MT 19:16–22 AND PROV 3:35–4:4

Another passage where modeling on an OT passage may explain Matthew's structure is the encounter between Jesus and the rich young man. This pericope has always been an important one in Synoptic criticism and because of the difficulty which surrounds the phrase, *εἷς ἐστιν ὁ ἀγαθός* in 19:17, it provides a test for the method of inquiry proposed here. Can a linear reading of Matthew's form of the story reveal why the story is presented in just this way?

A formal analysis of the Matthean pericope reveals a typical controversy story involving an exchange between Jesus and an interrogator. The limits of the passage are clear. In 19:16 the young man asks a question of Jesus, and in 19:22 the young man departs, the conversation ended. The debate can be outlined in a series of questions and answers.

Question:	Teacher, what good deed must I do, to have eternal life?
Counter-Question:	Why do you ask me about what is good?
Answer:	*εἷς ἐστιν ὁ ἀγαθός*. If you would enter life, keep the commandments.
Question:	Which ones?
Answer:	You shall not kill, You shall not commit adultery, You shall not steal, You shall not bear false witness, Honor your father and mother, and, You shall love your neighbor as yourself.
Question:	All these I have observed; what do I still lack?
Answer:	If you would be perfect, go, sell what you possess and give it to the poor, and you will have treasure in heaven; and come, follow me.

Every word of the direct discourse between Jesus and the young man is included in this outline. The structure of the passage is evident.

The formal clarity of the pericope is very nearly matched by logical clarity in the flow of thought. The basic theme of the dialogue is stated in the opening question, "What good deed is necessary for entrance into the New Age?"[41] At issue is the problem of ethical requirements for participation in the coming kingdom. Is it necessary for one to be a Pharisee? or an ascetic like John the Baptist? or sectarian with the Essenes? What is Jesus' prescription for conduct which will insure participation in the life of the age to come? The ensuing discussion establishes keeping the commandments as the basic criterion for the life of the age to come, but adds that if the young

41. *ζωήν* is understood as the life of the age to come. This passage, among others, is cited by Bauer-Arndt-Gingrich, *Lexicon*, 341, as an example of the exact eschatological use of the phrase.

man wishes to be perfect and to receive treasures in heaven, he should sell what he has, give the money to the poor, and follow Jesus. Although there is a logical leap from the question of life of the age to come to the concept of being perfect, the transition is provided for by the question, "What do I still lack?"[42]

Another way of approaching the thought of the passage is a study of the key concepts and their combination here. The passage discusses entrance into the life to come, the good, the commandments, and the perfect. How are these ideas brought together? Is there a history of discussion in which these ideas are connected? There is good evidence that this particular combination of ideas stems from Jewish discussions of the function of the Torah in connection with Prov 3:35–4:4.

In *Pirke Aboth* 6:3 the following passage is to be found:

> If David King of Israel, who learned but two things from Ahitophel, called him his teacher, his companion, and his familiar friend, how much more then must he that learns from his fellow a single chapter or a single Halakah or a single verse or a single expression or even a single letter pay him honour! *And *honour* is naught else than *the Law*, for it is written, "The wise shall inherit honour (Prov 3:35)," and "The perfect shall inherit good (Prov 28:10)"; and *good* is naught else than *the Law*, for it is written, "For I give you good doctrine; forsake ye not my Law (Prov 4:2)."[43]

The scriptural proof that honor is the Law (following the * in the text) is an obvious addition to the preceding argument about David and Ahitophel. The logic of the proof is easily followed.[44]

Premise A: The wise shall inherit honor (Prov 3:35).
Premise B: The perfect shall inherit good (Prov 28:10).
Conclusion A: Honor equals good.

Premise C: For I give you good doctrine;
Premise D: forsake ye not my Law (Prov 4:2).
Conclusion B: Good equals the Law.

Premise E (conclusion A): Honor equals good.
Premise F (conclusion B): Good equals the Law.
Conclusion C: Honor equals the Law.

It is apparent that an ingenious exegetical logic has been employed in order to establish that *Honor equals the Law.*

42. The logical and formal clarity of the Matthean version has been neglected in the critical treatment of the passage. Newer and more adequate treatments are now available in Trilling, *Das wahre Israel,* 192–194, and Davies, *The Setting of the Sermon on the Mount,* 210–213. Both have observed that the answers in vss. 17 and 21 are introduced in the same way (εἰ θέλεις) and are logically related to one another.

43. English translation, *The Mishnah,* by H. Danby, 459.

44. Danby, *The Mishnah,* 459, n. 2, recognizes the logical pattern.

All of the concepts which are central to the Matthean passage occur within this exegetical exercise: the good, the law, the inheritance (in Mt *the life to come*), and the perfect. Thus the *Aboth* tradition may prove of value in retracing the construction of the Matthean pericope.[45] The two passages are so distinct that literary dependence is impossible. The text of *Aboth* 6:3 provides firm evidence for an existing Jewish exegetical tradition which utilized the ideas found in Mt 19:16–22 in working with Prov 3:35–4:4 and 28:10.

How far is Mt 19:16–22 related to the Proverbs texts and to exegetical logic apparent in *Pirke Aboth* 6:3? The structure of Mt 19:16–19 can be followed almost completely from Prov 4:2 and 4:4. Both the initial question asked by the young man and the positive part of Jesus' reply may be derived from Prov 4:4.

> The opening question:
> What good thing must I do, to have eternal life?
> The basic reply:
> If you would enter into life, keep the commandments.
> Keep my commandments, and live (Prov 4:4).

A second relationship, the equation drawn from Prov 4:2 that the good equals the Law, helps us to return to the question which prompted this inquiry. How is the phrase **εἷς ἐστιν ὁ ἀγαθός** to be understood in Matthew? In view of the emerging connection with the Proverbs passage and with the *Pirke Aboth* discussion of the Torah, the suggestion once championed by C.C. Torrey that **ὁ ἀγαθός** means the Torah gains considerable strength.[46] The emphasis of the exchange between Jesus and the young man is upon the role of the Law. Jesus' answers directly cite the commandments. In this context the most natural reading of the problem phrase is, "One is the good," or "The Good is one." As in the Rabbinic equation, the good would be the Law. There is ample precedent in the Old Testament and in the Talmud for the Good (טוב) meaning either God or the Torah.[47] In its Matthean context the answer would mean that Jesus rejects the implication of the young man's question and reasserts the abiding validity of the Torah as the requirement for entrance into the life to come.

45. The problem of the date of the Rabbinic passage is both important and unimportant. Danby considers the whole sixth chapter of the *Aboth* to be a late gloss introduced for liturgical reasons (*The Mishnah,* 458, n. 12). On two counts, however, the tradition here cited is old. It is connected with R. Meir (c. 150) or R. Joshua b. Levi (c. 250) and appears also in the *Talmud, Berakoth* 5a. Moreover, since the equations are clearly appended to the topic under discussion because of the key word *honor,* the tradition may be very old. Further, as no dependence between Mt and *Aboth* is necessary but only a common exegetical tradition, the independence of the passages attests strongly to a common tradition behind both passages.

46. C. C. Torrey, *Our Translated Gospels,* 16.

47. For the meaning "Torah" see Dt 30:15, Ps 119:39, and the Rabbinic texts already cited. For the meaning God see *Berakoth* 9a, Ps 100:5; 25:8; and 34:8 as examples.

There are objections to such a translation, however. The normal way of translating a masculine substantive adjective in Greek is personal.[48] That is, one would expect the phrase to translate, "The good man is one." This strict rendering is untenable in the context and has prompted the more usual, "One there is who is good" (RSV), or "One alone is good" (NEB). Though these freer renderings do little to preserve sense in the context, they do provide grammatical sense. So the question now stands, "Can the grammatical objections to the translation in which the good is understood as the Law be met?"

An inquiry into the use of the substantive phrase, ὁ ἀγαθός, in the NT shows that it does not occur apart from this passage and its parallels. God is not called good at all and the attributive form is applied to Jesus only in Jn 7:12 by a puzzled crowd. Even in the Apostolic Fathers and the Apologists the substantive only occurs (also apart from reference to the pericope about the rich young man) with reference to God in I Clement 60:1.[49] It is evident that the substantive ὁ ἀγαθός in Mt 19:17 represents a unique case which cannot be decided simply by a grammatical rule.

Since neither the general rule for substantives nor Matthew's own use of substantives is helpful in this case, a more fruitful direction of inquiry may be a search for the possible referents of ὁ ἀγαθός in Matthew's terms. The major problem under discussion in the pericope is the role of the Law. Therefore, a survey of Matthew's use of terms related to the Law is in order. Wherever Matthew speaks of the Law in the generic sense equivalent to the concept of the Torah, he uses the masculine ὁ νόμος (5:17,18; 7:12; 11:13; 12:5; 22:36,40 and 23:23). Often the Law (ὁ νόμος) is used as the generic term in conjunction with further comment about the specific commandments (αἱ ἐντολαί) as in 5:19; 22:36,38,40.

In this light, the translation of εἷς ἐστιν ὁ ἀγαθός which most clearly fits the context of the pericope and accords most fully with other Matthean usage is, "The Good, that is, the Torah, is one." The generic term is indicated by the masculine adjective corresponding with the intended referent, ὁ νόμος. It is chosen to contrast with the narrower concept implied in the neuter singular τί ἀγαθόν of the young man's question. The proper translation of the initial exchange between the young man and Jesus is probably:

> "Teacher, what good thing must I do to have eternal life?" And he said to him, "Why do you ask me about what is good? The Good [the Torah] is one. If you would enter into life, keep the commandments."

This translation fits the logical requirements of the context exactly. It accords with Matthean usage concerning the Law. It utilizes the equation

48. In order to express a generic idea a neuter substantive would normally be used in Greek. See N. Turner, *Grammar of NT Greek*, III, 13–14.

49. This evidence is taken from E. Goodspeed, *Index Patristicus* (Leipzig: J. C. Hinrichs, 1907) and *Index Apologeticus* (Leipzig: J. C. Hinrichs, 1912).

which is derived from Prov 4:2 in *Pirke Aboth* 6:3, "the good equals the Torah."[50] It precedes a sentence which is a restatement of Prov 4:4. And it gives the answer required by the question. Jesus brings no new ethical command. There is just one Law, one Good, and it is the requirement for the life of the age to come, so keep the commandments.[51]

The linear analysis of the dialogue has now yielded some significant results. The problem phrase has been solved on Matthew's terms. A close relationship between the opening exchange of the dialogue and the application of Prov 4:2 and 4:4 to the Torah in Jewish exegesis has been made evident. The concepts of good, life, and the commandments are interrelated in a way which compels the conclusion that Mt 19:16–19 is closely related to Jewish discussion of Prov 4:2 and 4:4.[52]

The closing exchange of the dialogue raises almost as many questions for interpretation as does the opening one. To the young man's question, "I have done all this; what do I still lack?" Jesus replies with the counsel to perfection. The answer is formulated exactly as the previous one.

If you would enter life . . .

If you would be perfect . . .

But the formal affinity is deceptive. In the previous instance ground had been laid for the answer in the reference of the question to eternal life. Perfection has not been mentioned. Moreover, there was no hint in the earlier exchange that there was any limitation on the validity of the answer, "Keep the commandments." How does the argument move to the counsel to perfection?

The appearance of the term "to be perfect" in the passage in Matthew and in the series of equations in *Pirke Aboth* can scarcely be accidental. In *Aboth* 6:3 it is clear that the link is the combination of Prov 3:35 and 28:10. In the exegetical discussion of Torah, Prov 28:10 played a role by linking good and honor. The Matthean pericope reflects the adhesion of Prov 28:10

50. The equation drawn from Prov. 4:2 is more clear in Hebrew than in Danby's or the RSV's translations: כי לקח טוב נתתי לכם   תורתי אל-תעזבו

51. The objection of M. Smith in *Tannaitic Parallels to the Gospels* (JBL Monograph Series, VI. Philadelphia: Society of Biblical Literature, 1959), 33, that Torrey gave no adequate reason for reading ὁ ἀγαθός as a mistranslated הטוב or טבא is met here. Torrey was close to catching Matthew's intent, but it is not necessary to posit a mistranslation of Hebrew or Aramaic because a rationale for the masculine form can be found within Mt's Greek usage. This possibility was also seen by R. C. Haskins, "The Call to Sell All" (unpublished Ph.D. dissertation, Department of Religion, Columbia University, 1967), 22.

52. It should be noted that both the *Aboth* and the Matthean connections with Prov are dependent upon the Hebrew rather than the LXX text. Only Prov 4:2 of the four verses that are used gives the same sense in Hebrew and in the LXX. "And live" is absent from LXX Prov 4:4, and "the perfect shall inherit good" is absent from LXX Prov 28:10.

to the other passages in Proverbs but shows a different route of application. "The perfect shall inherit good" (Prov 28:10), is now taken literally. In the counsel given in Mt 19:21, the young man is urged to become perfect so as to have *treasure in heaven*. Thus, while the concept of perfection was probably linked to the discussion of the good in Jewish tradition by the exegetical formulas evident in *Aboth* 6:3, the Matthean pericope makes quite a different use of the connection with Prov 28:10.

The exegetical implication of the Matthean passage can scarcely be avoided. The passage does suggest a two-level approach to the life to come. At one level entrance is achieved simply by following the commandments, but at another level treasure is gained in heaven by heeding the counsel to perfection.[53] This is one of the passages in Matthew, along with 5:10–12; all of ch. 10; 25:31–46; and 28:16–20 (perhaps also 19:10–12 and 23–30), which give the impression that Matthew was written in part to bolster the morale of the disciples, the commissioned missionaries who carry the good news to all the nations. They must sacrifice and suffer, but glory awaits them in the new world when the Son of Man shall sit on his glorious throne (Mt 20:28; cf. 25:31 and 34).

The results of the application of linear analysis to this pericope may now be summarized. The dialogue is a question and answer debate. The major problem under discussion is the ethical requirement or requirements for entrance into the life to come. The concepts are utilized in conjunction with a traditional Jewish exegesis of Prov 3:35; 4:2; 4:4 and 28:10. In the use of terms related to the Law the passage is consistent with other Matthean passages. The counsel to perfection, adapted to this discussion and to Prov 28:10, is also reminiscent of Mt 5:48 (both instances are unique to Matthew). Two types of morality are clearly implied. The pericope may be read in linear fashion as a unified construction depending upon the traditional Jewish exegesis of the passages from Proverbs.

THE ANALYSIS AND FORM CRITICISM

While it would be tempting to suggest a break between vss. 19 and 20 and to assign the latter to Matthew or his church and the former part of the pericope to Jesus or the early church, neither the internal literary evidence (the parallels between vss. 17 and 21 suggest the contrary) nor the evidence from the Jewish exegetical tradition can support such a separation. The pericope is a unit in Matthew.

53. Although this challenges the position taken by Davies (*Setting*, 210–213), Barth (*Tradition and Interpretation*, 96–98), and Trilling, (*Das wahre Israel*, 192–194), the logic of the passage and the evidence from the parallels in *Aboth* and Prov seem to require the interpretation that two standards of morality are present in the text. As Haskins says, "It is undeniable, however, that, according to Matthew at this point, Jesus does imply a distinct dichotomy between the observance of the commandments and the renunciation of possessions, between entering life and being perfect" ("The Call to Sell All," 28).

More valuable for form critical consideration is the nature of the unit. The form, question and counterquestion, has now appeared in three Matthean passages relevant to this inquiry (the others were the Beelzebul controversy and the question about handwashing). In all three cases the form of the Matthean version is very exact. Either the question and counterquestion form of the controversy story is a favorite of Matthew (as it is of Jewish tradition), or it often belongs to the original tradition. The coincidence of this particular form with the passages amenable to redaction-critical study in Matthew should be explored further by someone interested in the formal character of the Synoptic controversy stories.

THE ANALYSIS AND MATTHEAN REDACTION

There is more and better evidence for the work of Matthew in this pericope than in the previous instances of pericopes modeled on OT passages. That evidence is 1) a consistency of viewpoint toward the validity of the Torah, 2) a consistency of terminology in speaking of the Law and the commandments, and 3) an application of the concept of perfection, which fits Matthew's view of total discipleship. Much of Mt 19 seeks to establish the radical requirements of discipleship, and this pericope fits into that context perfectly.

On the other hand, the evidence is not so strong as to be conclusive in favor of Matthean authorship. The debate over the validity of the Torah certainly has its origin in Jewish-Christianity but not necessarily with Matthew. It is possible that Matthew is in full accord with his source in this case and has followed it closely. The concepts and vacabulary are not uniquely Matthean as the parallel in *Aboth* 6:3 shows, but belong to Jewish tradition.

One factor may weigh in favor of Matthean construction to fit the special context of ch. 19. In 5:48, the counsel to perfection does not read as a counsel simply to the special disciples who have given up all to be Christ's emissaries. Rather, it stands as a general theological support for the ethic of non-retaliation. "God makes his sun shine on the just and on the unjust . . . . You must be perfect as your Father in heaven is perfect." The adaptation of the counsel to perfection to the discussion about the Torah diverges significantly from this general counsel and from the exegetical logic of *Aboth* 6:3. At the same time, it brings the pericope into close harmony with the thought of the surrounding context. Men must be eunuchs for the sake of the kingdom (19:12), and they must leave everything and follow (19:27). This would suggest conscious redactional application of the Torah debate to the context of the chapter through a special understanding of Prov 28:10.

On balance, the signs of Matthew's work in this pericope are significant. The passage reflects the Jewish-Christian milieu which has emerged elsewhere in the study as the background of Matthew's work. There are precise connections between Matthew's work in other portions of the gospel and in the immediate context with the ideas of this dialogue. Probability may rest with the conclusion that Matthew is largely responsible for the passage, but the strong possibility that a Jewish-Christian tradition is being utilized cannot be ruled out.

THE ANALYSIS AND THE SYNOPTIC PROBLEM

The discussion of the logical structure of Mt 19:16–22 which is derived from an exegetical use of Prov 3:35–4:4 and 28:10 brings new evidence to the discussion of literary dependence in this passage.

The difference between the Matthean version of the opening exchange and the Mark/Luke version has been explained by most scholars as strong evidence of Matthew's alleged tendency to alter his Marcan source for reverential reasons.[54] No plausible alternative explanation had ever been proposed.

The linear analysis has presented an alternative explanation of the structure of the Matthean pericope. The explanation of the debate in Matthew depends on evidence independent of source theory and especially of hypothetical motivation for alterations of one source by another. Therefore, the logical and formal unity of the Matthean passage emerges as a new factor in the discussion.

The key questions now seem to be: 1) Is it probable that Matthew found in the Mk/Lk version of the story the elements, though disjointed, which he needed for the construction of his dialogue on the Torah? or 2) Is it probable that Mark and/or Luke had difficulty with the grammatical shift from ἀγαθόν to ἀγαθός and proceeded to correct it, and in the process blurred the original structure? or 3) Does the version in Matthew represent his use of a tradition more primitive than that now found in Mark?[55]

Further inquiry is evidently needed into the structure of the Mk/Lk version of the debate and more adequate testing of the argument for

54. The following excerpt from the review of W. R. Farmer's *The Synoptic Problem* by F. W. Beare (*JBL* 84 [1965] 295–297) illustrates the argument for reverential change by Matthew. "On the strange variant between Mt. 19:17 and Mk. 10:18 ('Why do you ask me about what is good?—Why do you call me good?'), Farmer has nothing to say except that 'it is by no means certain that the text of Matthew is secondary to that of Mark or Luke' (p. 160). In fact, nothing is more certain; it is totally inconceivable that the Matthean form could arise except as a theologically motivated correction of the Markan text" (297). See in the same vein Streeter, *The Four Gospels*, 162; Bultmann, *The History of the Synoptic Tradition*, 357–358; and McNeile, *St. Matthew*, 277.

55. The similarity of the much shorter version in the Gospel of the Nazarenes as cited by Origen to that of Matthew may be some support for this third position. See J. Jeremias, *The Unknown Sayings of Jesus*, trans. by R. H. Fuller (2nd English ed.; London: SPCK, 1964), 43–47.

theological change by Matthew is in order.[56] Until this is done, this passage will not be useful as a latch-pin in any source theory.

SUMMARY

Mt 19:16–22 emerges through linear analysis as a dialogue constructed by use of arguments drawn from the exegesis of the Hebrew text of Prov 3:35; 4:2; 4:4 and 28:10. These parallels reveal the structure of the Matthean pericope and provide the logical thread which connects the elements of the story, especially the discussion of perfection. The place accorded the Torah in ethical requirement is fully in accord with Matthew's viewpoint as it emerges in the Sermon on the Mount. The counsel to perfection receives a novel twist which suits it for the theme of the demand for discipleship which governs ch. 19. Here is further evidence of Matthew's use of the OT and of Jewish exegetical traditions in an effort to define the Christian way. Matthew can be seen working as a Christian scribe familiar with the debates of Jewish tradition (even if he is utilizing rather than creating the tradition).

A SUMMARY OF THE RESULTS OF CHAPTER FOUR

The investigation of the possible use by Matthew of the OT in a third way, that of working model for gospel passages, has achieved mixed results.

It is clear that such modeling has occurred and that it can be demonstrated by cumulative and logical evidence in the case of all four Matthean passages. The origin of the modeling cannot be so easily fixed, however. In the case of the story of the Stilling of the Storm, the modeling very likely belongs to the originator(s) of the account in the early Palestinian church. The modeling is reflected in all of the Synoptic versions.

In the use of the Sinai motif for the transfiguration story, Matthew has preserved (or improved) the modeling to a large extent, but it is difficult to judge whether he originated the story or whether it belongs to an older Jewish-Christian tradition. The latter seems probable.

The use of Ps 22 in the crucifixion narrative presents the same kind of dilemma. Matthew's version is the most developed in its use of Ps 22, and the theology of the dying Messiah seems most at home in this gospel. Nonethe-

56. As far as I have been able to ascertain, the secondary evidence gives the theory of Matthean alteration of Mk little or no support. The supposedly theologically embarrassing Mk/Lk form was much preferred in the second century. The text tradition (which one would normally expect to be theologically reverent) assimilates Mt to Mk and Lk in this verse. This is the opposite of the normal movement of assimilation. (For the normal direction of assimilation see Streeter, *The Four Gospels,* 139.) In the second-century Fathers the Mk/Lk version is also clearly preferred (for example, Justin Martyr, *Apology I,* 16), and some correction of the Matthean form is made when it is used (Justin Martyr, *Dialogue with Trypho,* 101 and Irenaeus, *Against Heresies,* I, 20:2).

less, Matthew may reflect Jewish-Christian refinement of a process already evident in the Marcan passion narrative. All that can be said with certainty is that in Matthew the role of Ps 22 is explicit and that its use is vital to Matthew's presentation of Jesus.

The use of the Proverbs passages in the discussion of the good in 19:16–22 is more helpful in establishing Matthean redaction. The modeling, once seen, helps the reader to follow the Jewish logic of the dialogue and to understand the connection of perfection with the discussion of the good. The parallel Jewish tradition in *Aboth* 6:3 provides the necessary clue, but the method of connecting the Proverbs verses is one of standard Jewish exegesis, and the argument is older than the forms found in Matthew or *Aboth*. In this passage evidence of Matthean language and motif is stronger. The modeling, especially to suit the context in the gospel, is very likely the work of Matthew. For this pericope serious questions are raised for the theory that Matthew used Mark.

It is evident that there are instances where the OT serves as the model behind NT passages. There may well be others in Matthew for which I have not seen the clue which would open the model to critical view. The most important result of the chapter is the evidence that the method of linear analysis holds good for passages where the OT is used in this third way.

Finally, the chapter has furthered the search for the character of the redactor's work in Matthew by providing evidence of his familiarity with the OT (especially the Hebrew), with Jewish exegetical traditions, and with the milieu of Jewish-Christianity. Nothing has been found which would contradict, and much has been found which confirms, the working hypothesis that the author of the gospel of Matthew might be aptly described as a "scribe trained for the kingdom of heaven."

CHAPTER 5

CONCLUSIONS

Three basic ways in which a writer can employ a source in constructing his own document have now been explored in Matthew: direct citation and allusion, midterm application, and deliberate modeling. There may be other instances in Matthew where significant uses of the OT occur which have escaped attention, but the majority of Matthew's uses of the OT in structuring the gospel have certainly been considered. It remains to draw together the results of the inquiry.

1. The Basic Result: Evidence of the Conscious Use of the Old Testament in the Construction of the Gospel of Matthew.

The strongest new evidence gained concerning the work of Matthew comes from the study of his use of OT citations as the structural key to the composition of the passages in which they occur. Of the analyses in ch. 2, the mid-point use of the texts in 13:1–52, 12:9–50, 15:1–20, 10:35–37, and 11:9–15 is the most readily evident. The text in 9:13 may also serve as the structural key to 9:14–34.

The author's application of the OT in these cases varies. He employs Isa 6:9–10 in an allusive manner in 13:13–17 and then constructs the interpretation of the parable of the Sower from the allusion in keyword fashion. In 13:35 he uses Ps 78:2 in simple logical connection with his theory of parable interpretation. And the Elijah prophecy is also used in direct logical fashion in 11:9–15. In 12:22–37 the connections with the Isa 42 text are of the keyword variety, whereas in 15:10–20 the connections depend both upon the key words "mouth" and "heart" of the Isaiah text and also upon a special exegetical understanding of the OT passage. The illustration of the meaning of Mic 7:6 by means of a carefully constructed poetic couplet in 10:37 represents another way in which Matthew follows out an OT citation in the subsequent gospel text. If it is correct that 9:14–34 is governed by a special Matthean understanding of "I desire mercy and not sacrifice," then that passage represents still another means by which Matthew has employed the OT text as a structural key in his gospel.

The net result of the analyses of the mid-point texts is the discovery of the work of the gospel writer in weaving together the Jesus tradition and the OT, which serves him as scriptural authority. There is no longer any room for doubt that Matthew wrote in Greek and often employed the LXX, but, as in the exegesis in 15:10–20, at times a knowledge of the Hebrew text shines through his work. The imaginative variety in the connection between the Jesus tradition and the OT attests the author's skill and his profound familiarity with *both* traditions.

Evidence is abundant that these sections are the work of one author who utilized various traditions. A striking example is his use of a source containing paired kingdom parables in ch. 13. The recurrence of the exegetical phrase, "He who has ears, let him hear," in these mid-point passages (11:15; 13:9,43 and 15:10 "hear and understand") suggests self-conscious exegetical effort. The recurrence of themes, such as the importance of the spoken word (12:36–37; 15:10–20), the concept of treasure (12:35; 13:44 and 19:21), and hostility to the Pharisees (12:22–35; 15:12–14) not only links these sections of the gospel together, but also provides evidence of connection with other portions of the gospel. In addition, the literary variety of the material included in the mid-point sections (discourse 13:1–52; 10:34–37; controversy story 12:22–37,38–42; biographical narrative 12:46–50; miracles 9:18–34; 12:22–24; and a discussion of John the Baptist 11:9–15) renders unlikely any thought that all of these passages are taken from a single source. Some of the material is unique to Matthew (part of ch. 13), but much more is held in common with Mark and/or Luke. There can be little doubt that it was the author of Matthew who developed the mid-point passages.

In content the mid-point passages also reveal a measure of unity. The concerns are Jewish-Christian (eschatological exegesis of the parables, debate over Pharisaic rules, defense of Jesus' healing ministry, proof that Jesus is the promised Messiah and John the Baptist is the forerunner) and they are developed in typically Jewish fashion. A reading of the situation of the author from these passages must place him in the context of Jewish-Christianity which is engaged in intense controversy with Pharisaic Judaism.

The examination, in ch. 3, of other Matthean citations of or allusions to OT texts should be considered supplementary to the other evidence gained in the study. There is evidence of a variety of uses of OT texts, ranging from near mid-point (as in the story of the entry in 21:1–7) to a virtual ignoring of a traditional citation because of other interests (21:41–45). In general, these texts do not play decisive roles in the structure of the gospel. Only in the birth narrative is there any probability that an extensive deliberate construction in view of the OT passages has occurred. Because clues are lacking, it is often difficult to distinguish the author's use of the OT texts from applications that come to him in the tradition. In content, however, it remains true that the concerns and motifs which the texts reflect are Jewish-Christian: the messiahship of Jesus (1:23; 2:6), the prophet like Moses (2:15), John as the forerunner (3:3), and the fate of the betrayer seen through the eyes of prophecy (27:3–10). The use of the texts in citation and allusions supports the evidence gathered in the study of the mid-point texts about the overall character of the redaction by Matthew.

The evidence from the study in ch. 4 of passages which are modeled on OT narratives is also less clear than the evidence for mid-point construction. It is apparent that such modeling has taken place, but at what stage in the development of the tradition it originated is less clear. The study of the stilling of the storm indicates that this narrative was modeled on Jon 1 before the writing of the gospels. In the transfiguration and the crucifixion narratives, the Matthean version of the text shows the most precise modeling, but it is not clear whether this indicates that Matthew is solely responsible for the modeling or only for a refinement of it. Only in the dialogue with the rich young man is there sufficient evidence of interlocking Matthean motifs (and confusion in the corresponding Mk/Lk passages) to suggest that Matthew may be the one who molded the pericope, although the possibility cannot be excluded that some or even all of the modeling was done prior to Matthew.

Again the motifs of the passages coincide with those of the passages studied earlier. The crucifixion narrative reveals a Jewish-Christian effort to solve the scandal of a crucified Messiah by an application of Ps 22. The transfiguration draws parallels between the experience of Jesus and that of Moses on Sinai. And the dialogue with the rich young man takes up a basic question, "What is the Christian position vis-à-vis the Torah?" The precision of the modeling that is evident in Matthew and the awareness of Jewish exegetical tradition which shines through these passages, especially 19:16–22, confirm and support the view that the author of Matthew was a Jewish-Christian well trained in the use of the OT.

Summary The linear analysis of a number of passages in Matthew where evidence of redaction can be controlled through the use of the OT has produced the following results: 1) A largely successful tracing of the connective logic which governed the construction of the passages. 2) The discovery of considerable interplay of vocabulary and ideas among the passages concerned and with other portions of the gospel. 3) A demonstration of the markedly Jewish-Christian concerns of this author.

II. Results of the Study Which Concern Form and Source Criticism

In a few instances previous form-critical judgments have been called into question by the linear analyses. For example, the logical unity of the Matthean theory of parable interpretation raises some question as to whether the "blessing saying" (13:16–17) ever existed independent of its Matthean context and its allusions to Isa 6:9–10. In the main, however, no fundamental criticism of form criticism emerges from this inquiry.

One of the recurring instances of formal revision will deserve further attention. In three of the Matthean controversy stories (Beelzebul, handwashing, and rich young man), the form was question/counterquestion. The versions in Mark and Luke diverge from Matthew at this point. Does Matthew stylize the controversies in a Jewish-Christian fashion reminiscent of Rabbinic debates? Or, do Mark and Luke, unfamiliar with the Rabbinic debates, blur the original Jewish form? A further inquiry into the form of the controversy dialogues in Matthew appears to be in order.

For source criticism, the major result of this study will also bear further consideration. The cumulative evidence that the logic of the construction of major portions of Matthew can be traced provides new material for the study of the Synoptic problem. The linear logic of Matthew has never been considered in source-critical studies. When important elements of this redactional structure recur in the parallels in Mark and Luke, source critics are faced with a new problem. How shall they assess this evidence? Much more redactional work on Mark and Luke is necessary before any definite appraisal can be made.

III. RESULTS WHICH BEAR UPON THE SETTING OF THE GOSPEL

The goal of redaction-critical study is the reconstruction of the author's work in his setting. The analyses have focused on one aspect of Matthew's work, namely, his use of the OT in constructing the gospel. In the inquiry, evidence has been gathered which is important in assessing Matthew's situation.

It has already been noted that the research supports the view held by Stendahl, Kilpatrick, and Gundry that Matthew was able to utilize both the Greek and the Hebrew OT. The exegesis in 15:1–20 and the modeling in 19:16–22 are dependent upon knowledge of the Hebrew, but most of Matthew's other quotations reveal certain knowledge of the LXX: especially the citation of Isa 29:13 in Mt 15.

Matthew's exegetical use of the OT texts is fairly typical of first-century Jewish hermeneutics. He is prone to use catchwords to provide connections (12:22–50; 13:1–23). He can ignore the original context and meaning of a passage in order to draw from the text the meaning needed for his own purpose (the use of Isa 29:13 in 15:1–20 is the most obvious instance). In an important respect his use of the OT approaches most nearly the style of the scholars at Qumran: he may employ the standard Rabbinic hermeneutical techniques but in virtually every case he makes the OT text speak directly to the situation of Jesus or of the coming judgment. Bringing the text to bear so directly upon a historical moment is the major point at which Matthew's work parallels that of the writers of the Qumran *Pesharim*. The impetus for the work of both Matthew and the Qumran scribes is the firm belief that the writers are living in or near the days of the fulfillment of the OT promises. In this light, it is not surprising to find that Matthew is willing to bring the parables of Jesus, as well as OT prophecy, to bear on the events of the end-time (compare the theory of parables in Mt 13 as explained in ch. 2, Analysis 1).

When Matthew uses the OT text as the middle term for the construction of a gospel section, he is creating a new technique. The requirements of writing a gospel have meant for Matthew the task of drawing together into a unit the disparate elements available to him as Jesus tradition. The string which he provides for these beads is, in some significant cases, the OT citation or allusion and its subsequent connections with the gospel pericopes. It is apparent that this creative joining of the two traditions, the OT and the stories about Jesus, has been made by Matthew, whether or not he used Mark. The roots of Matthew's thought and technique may lie in first-century Judaism, but his creative skills are most evident in his inventive organization of the gospel.

When the search for the situation of the author moves beyond that of literary craft, judgments become more difficult. At numerous places in the analyses the reflection of Jewish or Jewish-Christian ideas in Matthew's work has been noted. The parables theory in ch. 13 is ingeniously developed from the Jewish concept of "mystery." The organization of 12:22–50 depends on keyword connections to a widely used Messianic text. The argument about collusion with Beelzebul employs Jewish logic and language to demolish the opponents. The application of the concept of the "forerunner" to John the Baptist in 11:9–15 requires a knowledge of that concept in Judaism. The formal and logical clarity of the debate about clean and unclean in ch. 15 shows that the author understood some of the subtlety of Rabbinic halakic tradition. The use of "mercy over sacrifice" as a means of explaining Jesus' non-kosher activity reflects one of the continuing dilemmas of Jewish-Christianity, namely, how far is the Torah (oral or written) binding on Christians? The same concern is at the base of the dialogue with the rich young man in 19:16–22. In the crucifixion narrative, Matthew reveals an awareness of the scandal for Jews and Jewish-Christians of a Messiah crucified by the Romans. In these and other ways, the ideas and motifs of the work of the redactor discovered in the linear analyses appear to be unmistakably those of a Jewish-Christian. In that respect this inquiry would support the opinion of the majority of scholars on the character of the author of Matthew.

More specific evidence of Matthew's situation may also be gained from the analyses. It was noted that 21:41–45 makes a clear reference to the destruction of Jerusalem. Thus, the gospel must have been written by a Jewish-Christian some time after 70 A.D. Unless Matthew was a refugee in a Gentile-Christian community, the book must have been written some time before the full effect of the adoption of the curse against the Christians (c. 85 A. D.) had isolated and separated Christianity from Judaism, that is, some time in the period 80–125 A.D.[1] Since this has been a generally accepted range of possibility for Matthew, the task is to narrow the options.

1. For a recent treatment of the institution of the 12th Benediction under R. Gamaliel II, see J. L. Martyn, *History and Theology in the Fourth Gospel*, 34–41. For its relevance to Mt see G.

The evidence from the linear analyses is not complete enough for one to speak with certainty on this issue. However, one feature of the study does bear directly on Matthew's standing in Judaism, the Beelzebul controversy. We know from Jewish tradition that one of the Jewish arguments against Christianity was the practice of magic.[2] Matthew's treatment of the charge is, therefore, revealing about his attitudes toward Judaism.

Matthew presents a doublet of the story of a healing of a demoniac followed by the Pharisaic charge, "He casts out demons by the prince of demons," in 9:32–34 and 12:22–24. In the latter case, utilizing the promise of the gift of the Spirit to the Messiah, Isa 42:1 // Mt 12:18, Matthew has constructed a scathing rebuke of the charge and of the Pharisees. In making this charge, according to Matthew, they blaspheme against the Spirit. Not only does this exchange reveal Matthew's own involvement in controversy with Pharisaic Judaism, but there is a third and even more telling reference to the Beelzebul charge. In 10:25, in the context of the mission charge and in a passage peculiar to Matthew, the charge recurs. "If they have called the master of the house Beelzebul, how much more will they malign those of his household?" This text can hardly mean anything other than that Matthew knows the Beelzebul charge by the Pharisees to be a genuine element in the wider controversy between his Christian community and its Pharisaic-Jewish neighbors. If so, Matthew must have been written in a time and for a church which was involved in a severe struggle with Pharisaic Judaism.

This conclusion has important consequences. The hostility expressed throughout Matthew against the Pharisees (cf. 15:12–14 and all of 23) is not a result of the anachronistic use of Jewish-Christian sources,[3] but is the direct result of the tensions between Matthew's church and Pharisaic Judaism. Consequently, Matthew must have been written either shortly before the adoption of the curse against the Christians when tensions were already mounting (as Hummel observes, there is no direct reference to the curse or expulsion from the synagogue in Matthew),[4] or shortly after while Jewish-Christianity was still a possibility and before a complete separation. On the other hand, Christians evidently were not members of Pharisaic synagogues, for Matthew seems to distinguish "their synagogues" as separate institutions.[5] The separation is under way. Pharisaic Judaism has not yet won full sway over Judaism in Matthew's area. Thus Matthew must be placed in the context of the painful time of separation of the church from

D. Kilpatrick, *The Origins of the Gospel According to St. Matthew* (Oxford: Clarendon Press, 1946), 109–111.

2. See Strack-Billerbeck, I, 631–635.

3. This position, taken by Hare in *The Theme of Jewish Persecutions of Christians*, 167–171, seems very insecure as a result of the analyses.

4. Hummel, *Die Auseinandersetzung*, 28–33.

5. Kilpatrick, *Origins*, 110–111.

Judaism which is also reflected in John's gospel. Because the hostility is not unrelieved by some admiration of the Pharisees (cf. 23:2), it is possible that Matthew's situation is less close to full separation than that of John.[6]

Two important considerations remain before this statement of Matthew's situation can be accepted. The evidence from the other analyses must be consulted. To my knowledge, there is nothing which has been gained in the linear analyses which contradicts such a picture of Matthew's situation and much that confirms it. A Jewish-Christian milieu, where hostile Pharisaic forces are operative, helps to account for the apologetic tone of much of Matthew's gospel, for example, 15:1–20. Moreover, it explains the distinct Jewishness of this gospel. Apparently Matthew's church recognizes and honors the Gentile mission, but it is not so "integrated" a community that racial slurs against Gentiles are always noticed as objectionable.

The analyses may lead a step further in analyzing the situation of Matthew, for in them some distinctive traits of Matthew and his Christian community are revealed. There is consistent evidence (in the parable discourse especially) for a full maintenance of an eschatological hope. Discipleship has become the key to the life to come (cf. 19:16–22), but there is no lessening of faith in the future consummation. Indeed, the judgment will come with Jesus as the judge (25:31–46), and those who have been faithful will be abundantly rewarded (19:21,28–29; 25:34). The emphasis on eschatology in Matthew may well reflect a church in conflict. It certainly does not contradict such a situation.

More interesting is the evidence of a genuine struggle in Matthew himself to maintain allegiance both to the Torah and to Jesus. No doubt Matthew believes in the rigor of Torah obedience as stated in 5:17–20, but he must come to grips with two real factors in his situation. First, the tradition about Jesus shows him to have been unorthodox in Torah observance (11:16–19 for example), and the open fellowship of the church with Gentiles strains Matthew's allegiance to Torah. As Tagawa has pointed out, it is not clear that Gentile-Christians would not be regarded by Matthew as having a new, basically Jewish identity.[7] But the evidence from the analyses shows Matthew justifying the breaking of Torah regulations on the principle of "I desire mercy and not sacrifice" (9:14–34) and on the principle of the priority of the intent of the heart over the external cleanliness of hands and lips (15:1–20). There is, therefore, good evidence of tension within Matthew himself over the crucial issue of first-century Judaism, Torah obedience. Matthew *wants* to honor the Torah, to claim a greater righteousness for Christians than for Pharisees (5:20), but he has not worked through the implications of the elements of the tradition from Jesus which lead to

6. On the situation of John and Judaism see again Martyn, *History and Theology in the Fourth Gospel.*

7. Tagawa, "People and Community," 161–162.

freedom from the Torah. Here, too, Matthew seems to stand on a bridge between Judaism and Christianity while the bridge is being torn asunder.

Before this statement of Matthew's situation can be accepted, however, some problematic passages need to be discussed. One text which appears to suggest a separation from Judaism is 21:43. However, as was noted above in the discussion of the passage (ch. 3), Trilling and Tagawa have a strong case that the saying, "Therefore I tell you, the kingdom of God will be taken from you and given to a nation producing the fruits of it," must be understoood both grammatically and in context as speaking of the taking of the kingdom from "the chief priests and the Pharisees" (vs. 45) and the giving of it to the church (sing. **ἔθνος**) rather than to the Gentiles (always plural **ἔθνη**).

Much more substantial objection to the situation proposed for Matthew results from another text which seems to speak of a rejection of the Jews as a people, 27:25. "And all the people answered, 'His blood be on us and on our children!'" This text seems to be a sweeping indictment of Judaism for the death of the Messiah. How could it have been written by a Jewish-Christian?

But further investigation raises questions for this traditional understanding of the verse. In a parallel passage, Luke also shows an interest in the innocence of the Romans, but has no corresponding condemnation of the Jews. In its place stands a dire prophecy:

> Daughters of Jerusalem, do not weep for me, but weep for yourselves and for your children. For behold the days are coming when they will say, "Blessed are the barren, and the wombs that never bore" (Lk 23:28f.).

The passage is probably a reference to the fall of Jerusalem as a judgment for the crucifixion of Jesus.[8]

It is also clear from Mt 21:41–45 that Matthew understands the destruction of Jerusalem in 70 as a judgment upon those in Judaism who were responsible for the death of Jesus.[9] Is it possible that the text in 27:25 is similarly directed? The initial difficulty with such a suggestion would be that the acceptance of the blood guilt appears to be hereditary for all coming generations. However, I have been unable to discover any reference in the OT or Rabbinic sources which speaks of "the children" or "our children" in a sense other than the generation named unless there is some qualifying phrase such as "to the end of the age." The parallels cited in Strack-Billerbeck bear out this suggestion fully. The blood guilt is always made precise upon the persons intended unless a qualifying phrase is used to indicate progeny.[10]

In the Lucan passage the mothers of Jerusalem and their children are to be pitied. They are exactly those who would have perished in Jerusalem 40

8. Cf. Creed, *St. Luke,* 285–286.

9. See Hummel's excellent treatment of this passage, *Die Auseinandersetzung,* 84ff., and the analysis above, ch. 3, pp. 85f.

10. Strack-Billerbeck, *Kommentar,* I, 1033. See also H. Graf Reventlow, "Seine Blut komme über sein Haupt," *VT* 10 (1960) 311–327.

years later. The same is true in Matthew. The crowd, the authorities, and all the people of Jerusalem accept the risk of blood guilt upon themselves and their children. The offense is clear. They are bearing false witness against an innocent man. The penalty for false witness was the punishment sought for the innocent (Dt 19:18–19). It seems likely that, in the context of the trial of Jesus, the acceptance of guilt by the people clamoring for Jesus' death is understood by Matthew as the genuine cause for the tragedy of 70 A.D. and further evidence of the validity of the Christian claim to messiahship for Jesus. Taking the text to mean that Matthew imputes guilt upon all Jews for all time reads far more into the text than the words or the context allow.

Mt 27:25 read in the light of 21:41–45 and Lk 23:28f. is understandable from the pen of a Jewish-Christian author or tradition and probably only so. It utilizes the Jewish concept of blood guilt for the illegal execution of an innocent man. This concept is Jewish, not Roman or Greek. It places that guilt on precisely two generations of the inhabitants of Jerusalem and their leaders. Thus it is firmly in accord with the Jewish-Christian explanation of the catastrophe that the destruction of Jerusalem represented for all Judaism. Jerusalem fell because of the crucifixion of Jesus. In her destruction and burning the penalty for that blood guilt was exacted. A Jewish-Christian author uses this argument to call for repentance and belief in Jesus the Messiah, to discredit the leadership of the Pharisees, but not to place a stigma of guilt upon himself and his people. Only in the light of the later complete separation of the church from Judaism was this last argument given prominence.

Another verse in Matthew, 28:15, causes some difficulty for the view that the gospel is written by a Jewish-Christian. In the discussion about the contrived Jewish explanation for the disappearance of Jesus' body from the tomb, the conclusion reads: "And this story has been spread among the Jews (Ἰουδαῖοι) until this day." This is the only instance in the gospel of Matthew where Ἰουδαῖοι is used by the author as though the persons named were distinct from him and his community. In each of the other instances of its use in Matthew the term is used by Gentiles of Jews, in accord with common usage (2:2; 27:11,29,37).

Perhaps there is no satisfactory explanation for this verse if it were written by a Jewish-Christian author. However, it has a strong parallel in the consistent use of Ἰουδαῖοι by the author of the Fourth Gospel, who was probably a Jewish-Christian (Jn 3:1; 4:9,22; 6:10; 9:48 and elsewhere). Perhaps in Matthew's Christian community the name "Jews" could also be applied in a negative sense for the opponents as a hostile religious community. At any rate the story in which the verse occurs is a manifestly Jewish tradition, one found only in Matthew. Perhaps Matthew knew that the story was widespread and could not be assigned solely to the major opponents, the Pharisees. As a popular rumor, perhaps it could only be assigned to Jews in general.[11] But the fact that the story is Jewish and deals with a specifically Jewish denial of the resurrection points to its origin in a Jewish versus Jewish-Christian controversy. Even though it is a puzzling verse, it is easier to assign it to a Jewish-Christian redactor than to any other.

There are, then, no insurmountable difficulties for the view that Matthew was written by a Jewish-Christian who belonged to a church which was already separated from Pharisaic Judaism and in sharp conflict with Pharisaism. The Christian fellowship probably included Gentiles (although precise evidence is lacking) but prided itself in being more faithful to the intent of the Torah (5:17–20; 12:1–21) than the Pharisees were. They hoped for the return of Jesus, the Messiah, as the Son of Man who would judge the nations (25:31-46). They believed in and supported the mission to "all the nations" (28:19). This picture of the situation of Matthew as drawn from the linear analyses is largely in accord with that proposed by R. Hummel, W. D. Davies, and G. D. Kilpatrick.[12] I think it is the clearest reading of the available evidence.

IV. A RETURN TO THE WORKING HYPOTHESIS

This study of the structural role played by the use of the OT in Matthew began as an effort to formulate and test a method for redaction-critical inquiry. Its purpose was to examine those passages where the writer of the gospel may have used the OT as a vehicle for constructing his gospel story. The linear analyses have borne enough fruit to substantiate the validity of the method of approach and have also provided confirmation of the working hypothesis which provided the special way of seeing, the particular critical slant for entering the gospel of Matthew.

Thus the overall effect of this study is confirmation of the initial hypothesis.

The author of Matthew was a Jewish-Christian so thoroughly familiar with the OT and with Jewish traditions of its interpretation that it was natural for him often to employ this knowledge as a key to the organization of his gospel. Where he has done this, he reveals to the reader certain of his characteristic ideas and beliefs. He also reveals his understanding of the relationship between the tradition about Jesus and the OT and the relationship of both to the problems of Christians of his own day. He probably thought of himself as "a scribe trained for the kingdom of heaven."

11. For a discussion of the charge and countercharge see H. F. von Campenhausen, "The Events of Easter and the Empty Tomb," in *Tradition and Life in the Church*, trans. by A. V. Littledale (Philadelphia: Fortress Press, 1968), 64–69.

12. R. Hummel, *Die Auseinandersetzung*, 26–33; W. D. Davies, *The Setting*, 256–315; G. D. Kilpatrick, *The Origins*, 101–123.

BIBLIOGRAPHY

Books

Allen, W. C. *The Gospel According to St. Matthew*. 3rd ed. Edinburgh: T. & T. Clark, 1912.

Bauer, W.; Arndt, W. F. and Gingrich, F. W. *A Greek-English Lexicon of the New Testament*. Chicago: University of Chicago Press, 1957.

Bellinzoni, A. J. *The Sayings of Jesus in the Writings of Justin Martyr*. Leiden: E. J. Brill, 1967.

Bentzen, A. *King and Messiah*. Napierville, Ill.: A. R. Allenson, 1954.

Betz, O. *Offenbarung und Schriftforschung in der Qumransekte*. Tübingen: J. C. B. Mohr, 1960.

Beyer, K. *Semitische Syntax im Neuen Testament*. Vol. 1. Göttingen: Vandenhoeck and Ruprecht, 1962.

Black, M. *An Aramaic Approach to the Gospels and Acts*. Oxford: Clarendon Press, 1954; [3]1967.

Borgen, Peder. *Bread From Heaven*. Leiden: E. J. Brill, 1965.

Bornkamm, G. *Jesus of Nazareth*. Translated by I. and F. McCluskey with J. Robinson. New York: Harper and Row, 1960.

Bornkamm, G.; Barth, G.; Held, H. C. *Tradition and Interpretation in Matthew*. Translated by P. Scott. London: SCM Press, 1963.

Brown, R. E. *The Gospel of John*. Vol. 1. *The Anchor Bible*. New York: Doubleday, 1966.

Brown, R. E. *The Semitic Background of the Term "Mystery" in the New Testament*. Philadelphia: Fortress Press, 1968.

Bultmann, R. *Das Evangelium des Johannes*. 18th printing of the 1941 original. Göttingen: Vandenhoeck and Ruprecht, 1964.

Bultmann, R. *The History of the Synoptic Tradition*. Translated by John Marsh. Oxford: Basil Blackwell, 1963.

Bultmann, R. *Jesus and the Word*. Translated by L. Smith and E. Lantero. New York: Charles Scribner's Sons, 1958.

Butler, B. C. *The Originality of St. Matthew*. Cambridge: Cambridge University Press, 1951.

Cadbury, H. J. *The Making of Luke-Acts*. 2nd ed. London: SPCK, 1958.

Conzelmann, Hans. *The Theology of St. Luke*. Translated by G. Buswell. London: Faber & Faber, 1960.

Creed, J. M. *The Gospel According to St. Luke*. New York: St. Martin's Press, 1965.

Dalman, G. *The Words of Jesus*. Translated by D. Kay. Edinburgh: T. & T. Clark, 1902.

Davies, W. D. *The Setting of the Sermon on the Mount*. Cambridge: Cambridge University Press, 1964.

Dibelius, M. *From Tradition to Gospel.* Translated by B. L. Woolf. New York: Charles Scribner's Sons, 1965.

Dodd, C. H. *The Parables of the Kingdom.* Revised ed. New York: Charles Scribner's Sons, 1961.

Engnell, I. *Studies in Divine Kingship in the Ancient Near East.* 2nd ed. Oxford: Blackwell's, 1967.

Farmer, W. R. *The Synoptic Problem.* New York: Macmillan, 1964.

Fuller, R. *The New Testament in Current Study.* New York: Charles Scribner's Sons, 1962.

Gnilka, J. *Die Verstockung Israels.* München: Kösel-Verlag, 1961.

Goodspeed, E. J. *Index Apologeticus.* Leipzig: J. C. Hinrichs, 1912.

Goodspeed, E. J. *Index Patristicus.* Leipzig: J. C. Hinrichs, 1907.

Gundry, R. *The Use of the Old Testament in St. Matthew's Gospel.* Leiden: E. J. Brill, 1967.

Haenchen, E. *Die Apostelgeschichte. Meyers Kommentar.* Göttingen: Vandenhoeck & Ruprecht, 1961.

Hare, D. R. A. *The Theme of Jewish Persecution in the Gospel According to St. Matthew.* Cambridge: Cambridge University Press, 1967.

Hummel, R. *Die Auseinandersetzung zwischen Kirche und Judentum im Matthäusevangelium.* München: Chr. Kaiser Verlag, 1963.

Jeremias, J. *The Parables of Jesus.* Translated by S. Hooke. Revised ed. New York: Charles Scribner's Sons, 1962.

Jeremias, J. *The Unknown Sayings of Jesus.* Translated by R. H. Fuller. 2nd English ed. London: SPCK, 1964.

Käsemann, E. *Exegetische Versuche und Besinnungen.* 2nd ed. Göttingen: Vandenhoeck and Ruprecht, 1960.

Kilpatrick, G. D. *The Origins of the Gospel According to St. Matthew.* Oxford: Clarendon Press, 1946.

Kingsbury, J. D. *The Parables of Jesus in Matthew 13.* London: SPCK, 1969.

Klausner, J. *The Messianic Idea in Israel.* New York: The Macmillan Co., 1955.

Lindars, B. *New Testament Apologetic.* London: SCM Press, 1961.

Lohmeyer, Ernst. *Das Evangelium des Matthäus.* Edited by W. Schmauch. Göttingen: Vandenhoeck and Ruprecht, 1962.

Mann, J. *The Bible as Read and Preached in the Old Synagogue.* Vol. 2. Cincinnati: Hebrew Union College, 1966.

Manson, William. *Jesus the Messiah.* Philadelphia: Westminister Press, 1946.

Martyn, J. L. *History and Theology in the Fourth Gospel.* New York: Harper and Row, 1968.

Marxsen, Willi. *Der Evangelist Markus. Studien zur Redaktionsgeschichte des Evangeliums.* Göttingen: Vandenhoeck and Ruprecht, 1956.

Marxsen, Willi. *Mark the Evangelist.* Translated by Roy A. Harrisville [*et al.*]. Nashville: Abingdon Press, 1969.

McNeile, A. H. *The Gospel According to St. Matthew*. New York: St. Martin's Press, 1965.

Metzger, B. *The Text of the New Testament*. Oxford: Clarendon Press, 1964.

Montefiore, C. G. *The Synoptic Gospels*. Vol. 1. 2nd ed., revised. New York: Macmillan, 1927.

Mowinckel, Sigmund. *He That Cometh*. Translated by G. W. Anderson. New York: Abingdon Press, 1954.

Perrin, Norman. *Rediscovering the Teaching of Jesus*. London: SCM Press, 1967.

Perrin, Norman. *What is Redaction Criticism?* Philadelphia: Fortress Press, 1969.

Rohde, Joachim. *Rediscovering the Teaching of the Evangelists*. Translated by Dorothea Barton. London: SCM Press, 1968.

Sanders, E. *The Tendencies of the Synoptic Tradition*. Cambridge: Cambridge University Press, 1969.

Schlatter, Adolf. *Das Evangelium nach Matthäus: Erlauterungen zum Neuen Testament*. Band I. Stuttgart: Calwer Verlag, 1961.

Singer, I., ed. *The Jewish Encyclopedia*. 12 vols. New York: Funk and Wagnalls, 1901-1906.

Smith, M. *Tannaitic Parallels to the Gospels*. *Journal of Biblical Literature* Monograph Series. Vol. VI. Philadelphia: Society of Biblical Literature, 1951.

Stendahl, K. *The School of St. Matthew*. 2nd ed. Philadelphia: Fortress Press, 1968.

Strack, Hermann. *Introduction to Talmud and Midrash*. 2nd ed. New York: Harper and Row, 1965.

Strack, H. L. and Billerbeck, P. *Kommentar zum Neuen Testament aus Talmud und Midrasch*. 6 vols. München: C. H. Beck, 1922–61.

Strecker, G. *Der Weg der Gerechtigkeit*. 2nd ed. Göttingen: Vandenhoeck & Ruprecht, 1966.

Streeter, B. H. *The Four Gospels*. London: Macmillan and Co., Inc., 1924.

Taylor, V. *The Gospel According to St. Mark*. London: Macmillan and Co., Ltd., 1963.

Thompson, Wm. G., *Matthew's Advice to a Divided Community*. Rome: Biblical Institute Press, 1970.

Torrey, C. C. *Our Translated Gospels*. New York: Harper & Brothers, 1936.

Trilling, W. *Das wahre Israel*. 2nd ed. München: Kösel-Verlag, 1964.

Turner, N. *Grammar of New Testament Greek*. Vol. 3. Edinburgh: T. & T. Clark, 1963.

Von Rad, G. *Genesis*. Translated by J. H. Marks. Philadelphia: Westminister Press, 1961.

Von Rad, G. *Studies in Deuteronomy*. Translated by G. Stalker. London: SCM Press, 1953.

Von Rad, G. *The Theology of the Old Testament*. 2 Vols. Translated by G. Stalker. New York: Harper Brothers, 1962.

Weiss, J. *Das älteste Evangelium*. Göttingen: Vandenhoeck & Ruprecht, 1903.

Wellhausen, J. *Das Evangelium Marci*. Berlin: 1909.

Westermann, C. *The Praise of God in the Psalms*. Translated by K. R. Crim. Philadelphia: John Knox Press, 1965.

Wink, Walter. *John the Baptist in the Gospel Tradition*. Cambridge: Cambridge University Press, 1968.

Winter, Paul. *On the Trial of Jesus*. Berlin: DeGruyter, 1961.

Articles

Beare, F. W. Review of *The Synoptic Problem*, by W. R. Farmer. *JBL* 84 (1965) 295–297.

Buchanan, G. W. "Some Vow and Oath Formulas in the New Testament." *HTR* 58 (1965) 319–326.

Cope, L. "Matthew 25:31–46, 'The Sheep and the Goats' Reinterpreted." *Nov T* 11 (1969) 32–44.

Daube, D. "Public Retort and Private Explanation." *The New Testament and Rabbinic Judaism*. London: University of London, Athlone Press, 1956, 141–157.

Davis, C. "Tradition and Redaction in Matthew 1:18–2:23." *JBL* 90 (1971) 404–421.

Davison, J. "The Homeric Question." *A Companion to Homer*. Edited by Wace and Stubbings. London: Macmillan, 1962, 234–268.

Dibelius, M. "Style Criticism of the Book of Acts." *Studies in the Acts of the Apostles*. Translated by Mary Ling. London: SCM Press, 1956, 1–25.

Dupont, J. "Les Paraboles du sénevé et du levain." *NRT* 89 (1967) 897–913.

Easton, B. S. "The Beelzebul Actions." *JBL* 32 (1913) 57–73.

Evans, O. "The Unforgivable Sin." *ExpT* 68 (1957) 240–244.

Farmer, W. R. "The Lachmann Fallacy." *NTS* 15 (1968) 441–442.

Fitzmyer, J. "The Aramaic Qorban Inscription from Jebel Hallet Et-Turi and Mk 7:11/Mt 15:5." *JBL* 78 (1959) 60–65.

Foerster, W. "Δαίμων." *TDNT* (1964) 1–21.

Gärtner, B. "The Habbakuk Commentary and the Gospel of Matthew." *ST* 8 (1954) 1–24.

Gerhardsson, B. "The Parable of the Sower and its Interpretation." *NTS* 14 (1968) 165–193.

Gese, H. "Psalm 22 und das Neue Testament." *ZTK* 65 (1968) 1–22.

Jeremias, J. "Παῖς Θεοῦ." *TDNT* 5 (1967) 677–717.

Jeremias, J. "Ελείας" *TDNT* 2 (1967) 930–943.

Johnson, S. "The Biblical Quotations in Matthew." *HTR* 36 (1943) 135–153.

Kuhn, K. G. "The Two Messiahs of Aaron and Israel." *The Scrolls and the New Testament*. Edited by K. Stendahl. New York: Harper and Brothers, 1957, 54–64.

Kümmel, W. G. "Jesus und der jüdische Traditionsgedanke." *ZNW* 33 (1934) 122–123.

Lohmeyer, E. "Die Verklärung Jesu nach dem Markusevangelium." *ZNW* 16 (1922) 185–215.

Michaels, J. R. "Apostolic Suffering and Righteous Gentiles." *JBL* 84 (1965) 27–37.

Reventlow, H. Graf. "Seine Blut komme über sein Haupt." *VT* 10 (1960) 311–327.

Roberts, B. J. "The Dead Sea Scrolls and the Old Testament Scriptures." *BJRL* 36 (1953) 75–96.

Robinson, J. A. T. "The Parable of the Sheep and the Goats." *NTS* 2 (1955–56) 225–237.

Rosche, T. R. "The Words of Jesus and the Future of the 'Q' Hypothesis." *JBL* 79 (1960) 210–220.

Sanders, E. "The Argument from Order and the Relationship between Matthew and Luke." *NTS* 15 (1968) 249–261.

Stein, R. H. "What is Redaktionsgeschichte?" *JBL* 88 (1969) 45–56.

Tagawa, K. "People and Community in the Gospel of Matthew." *NTS* 16 (1970) 149–162.

Taylor, G. "The Function of Pistis Christou in Galatians." *JBL* 85 (1966) 58–76.

Torrey, C. C. "The Biblical Quotations in Matthew." *Documents of the Primitive Church.* New York: Harper and Brothers, 1941, pp. 41–90.

Via, D. O. "Matthew on the Understanding of the Parables." *JBL* 84 (1965) 430–432.

Von Campenhausen, Hans. "The Events of Easter and the Empty Tomb." *Tradition and Life in the Church.* Translated by A. Y. Littledale. Philadelphia: Fortress Press, 1968, 42–89.

Wilkens, W. "Die Redaktion des Gleichniskapitels Mark. 4 durch Matth." *TZ* 20 (1964) 305–327.

Wood, H. G. "The Priority of Mark." *ExpT* 65 (1953–54) 17–19.

Unpublished Material

Haskins, R. C. "The Call to Sell All." Unpublished Ph.D. dissertation, Department of Religion, Columbia University, 1967.

Texts

Danby, H. *The Mishnah.* London: Oxford University Press, 1967.

Mekilta De Rabbi Ishmael. Translated by J. Z. Lauterbach. Philadelphia: Jewish Publication Society of America, 1933.

Migne, J. P., ed. *Patrologiae Cursus Completus—Series Graeca.* Vol. 6. Paris: 1857.

Roberts and Donaldson, ed. *The Ante-Nicene Fathers.* Vol. 1. American edition revised by A. C. Coxe. Grand Rapids: Wm. B. Eerdmans, 1950.

Gaster, T. H. *The Dead Sea Scriptures.* New York: Doubleday and Company, Inc., 1956.

INDEX OF MODERN AUTHORS

INDEX OF BIBLICAL REFERENCES

Matthew (Cont'd)